This book is dedicated to my parents, Carmen Gorina and Joan de Molina, to whom I owe everything. They have taught me a sense of family from childhood. I would also like to thank my siblings, who have always been close to me despite the physical distance.

Dr. Karl-Maria de Molina, Editor

Dr. Karl-Maria de Molina, Editor

The *Renaissance* of the *Family*
A practical guide for families

This book is published as part of the Family Valued project
(www.FamilyValued.org)

The German version was published at the end of November 2024,
and at the End of 2025 follows the Spanish version.

Bibliografische Information der Deutschen Nationalbibliothek: Die Deutsche Nationalbibliothek verzeichnet diese Publikation in der Deutschen Nationalbibliografie; detaillierte bibliografische Daten sind im Internet über http://dnb.dnb.de abrufbar.

Lektorat: Peter Brittain, Andrea Kitzelmann, Claus Schulte-Uebing

Cover Design Fotini Theodosiou

Verlag: BoD · Books on Demand GmbH, In de Tarpen 42, 22848 Norderstedt,
bod@bod.de

Druck: Libri Plureos GmbH, Friedensallee 273, 22763 Hamburg

ISBN: 978-3-7693-2241-5

Table of Contents

1 Preface

Family — the concept we once took for granted has now become a deliberate choice. Today, the decision to start a family is more complex than ever. Those who choose to embark on this journey face numerous challenges and decisions that simply didn't exist in the same way just a few decades ago.

When I became a mother, I was very young. At that time, none of my peers had children, and my husband and I often felt adrift, searching for role models to guide us. Reflecting back now, I realize that no one ever told us how enriching and fulfilling it could be to have a large family. We weren't prepared for the immense joy and the wonderful experiences that would come from raising our children. Nor were we fully supported as we navigated the many challenges of family life and partnership. Yet, looking back, I can say that my seven children are my greatest blessing. I often worried that raising a family would hold back my career. But now, I see how invaluable the skills I gained through motherhood—such as stress management, conflict resolution, task coordination, leadership, and visionary thinking—have been both in my professional and personal life.

Today's society is increasingly focused on the individual. In the Western world, we have more choices than ever before about how we live our lives. Yet, the flip side of this abundance of choice is a growing sense of isolation. We see this every day: loneliness is on the rise, intergenerational contact is dwindling, older adults often live alone in anonymous care facilities, the number of single households is increasing, and dating has become less committed in the age of social media.

At the same time, the traditional image of the family is fading. But what does "traditional" mean today? Is it merely the classic model of mother, father, and child, or is it about creating a strong, intergenerational bond? What does a modern family look like in today's world? In a society that places such a high value on individuality, family life has become a complex endeavour, requiring a balance between each member's unique qualities and the shared values that are the foundation of family.

In recent decades, the concept of family has been undervalued, and it's time for a renaissance. This revival should make space for individual growth while also reaffirming the immense value of a strong family structure for parents, children, and society as a whole. Without the family, which has been the cornerstone of social structure for centuries, it's hard to imagine a future that is truly worth living.

It's time to bring the family back into focus! The following chapters explore the family from various perspectives and consider how its future can be shaped. It's a task for all of us to undertake!

Prof. Julia Finkeissen

More info about the author via the QR code:
www.familyvalued.org/Julia-Finkeissen-2

2 Introduction

Why have 44 authors decided to address such a plain old topic as The Family? What is new about this book? In view of how much has already been written on the subject, do we need it at all?

Notwithstanding their different perspectives on the family, one thing unites all these authors, and that is their deep appreciation for it. Our joint mission is to put the spotlight on "a rediscovery of the family and its importance for society".

Although most of the authors and readers come from the German-speaking regions of Europe, we have included contributions from other countries, in order to broaden the perspective and so enrich the collection.

This book is part of the international project, "**Family Valued**" — an ecosystem consisting of a book, a homepage and a social media platform, all interlinked. The ecosystem approach makes the book interactive, so to speak, by expanding it to online content: author profiles, texts, videos, podcasts and others. Its multidimensionality gives the book a unique dynamic, improving the reader's "customer journey" and rendering the articles livelier and more immediate. Due to its international audience, the book is in both German and English. And later 2025 in Spanish.

The "**Family Valued**" project aims to "strengthen the self-confidence of families", hence our motto: "Making families stronger". In our opinion, this is necessary because the family is under attack from different sides and ideologies.

The book is a mosaic in that we look at different aspects of the family, and from different perspectives. First, we discuss its importance, indeed its necessity, for society. Then, since the book addresses families of working people, the compatibility of family and career comes second; and because the couple's relationship forms the backbone of the family, that topic is placed here, too. This is followed by children and their upbringing. As our Western society is ageing, caring for sick and disabled relatives is an important part of our lives. We have therefore dedicated a chapter to it. Finally, we share advice from families in the form of "best practices".

All the above topics could all be labelled "challenges for families". Therefore, the format of the articles is to describe those challenges and then point out practical countermeasures. Hence the book can be considered a self-help guide for families.

As stated above, the book is only one part of the overall "**Family Valued**" project. Over the next 5 years we aim to publish a lot more articles and encouraging news on the homepage, then link them to the authors' social media channels so that an active and lively community can develop.

And let us not forget that everything costs money. Therefore, the community of authors and readers has joined forces with donors. Donations are collected by the Familienglueck.de Foundation. We would also like to thank the Heimer family for including the project in their foundation.

The "**Family Valued**" team would like to thank all authors, who submitted and revised their contributions in careful, painstaking work.

And as editor, I would also like to thank everyone in the team who made this project possible, and especially Peter Brittain for the English editing, Andrea Kinzelmann for correcting the texts and Raúl Sánchez for suggestions and the mediation of contacts with authors.

I would like to conclude this introduction with a quote from the book "Future Family" by our author Ana Hoffmeister: "*The diverse personal insights in this book are embedded in the overarching question of how we will shape family, work and life in the future. How we can live together, who is part of our family life, how the status of family in our society can change and what it takes to do so.*"

Dr. Karl-Maria de Molina, Editor

More info about the author via the QR code:
www.familyvalued.org/Karl-Maria-de-Molina-2

3 Family and Society

Dr. Ana Hoffmeister
Consultant and author
Germany

The Family between change and increase in value

Abstract
Whether it's a kindergarten strike, a school failure or a "daycare-tastrophe": families can rely decreasingly on institutional support. They are increasingly at the end of your tether in everyday life between work, care and private life, and feel abandoned by the state. Nevertheless, families are indispensable for a sustainable society. In the search for alternative support systems and work models, new life plans are emerging, and the image of the family is changing.

Article
For most Germans, family is life's most valued possession – even above work, friends and hobbies. And not only for parents with underage children, but also for the young generation, which sees the family as a source of meaning and orientation.

Family has been at the core of our social life for centuries and has always been more than just the connection between mother, father and child. Family connects generations into a common story. It gives insights into our past and our common future. Family is the place where elementary questions about our origins, identity and belonging are shaped and answered. What we experience in our families is formative for all other relationships in life – whether in a professional context or in

voluntary work, whether in our friendships, our partnership or in the family we start ourselves.

"In the next few years, families worldwide will shrink by 35%".

In view of the current crises in politics, the economy, society and the climate, we have in recent years experienced a profound loss of public confidence in the effectiveness of political action. In the course of these developments, families are gaining importance as a stabilizing force and are an important social safety net that is taking considerable additional strain. Whether it's the daycare crisis, wretched schooling or our ailing care system, families are increasingly absorbing the state's deficiencies and are increasingly reaching their limits. The number of parents suffering from burnout continues to rise even after the pandemic, and mental illnesses among children and adolescents also continue to increase. The pressing question is therefore whether our current family structures are strong enough to be able to offer this essential social and emotional support in the future.

"The way we live as a family today inevitably shapes future generations".

In the next few years, families worldwide will shrink by 35 %. We will have fewer relatives overall than our ancestors. This will further increase the pressure on institutional support systems. This is because relatives – whether grandparents, aunts and uncles – already absorb a large proportion of childcare and private care and are therefore an important pillar in the compatibility of family and career. Our society is getting older and with it the age range of generations continues to grow. Grandchildren will probably have more living grandparents in the future – but the question will be whether these will still be fit enough to take care of their grandchildren. While Germany is struggling with falling birth rates and politics that are often perceived as child-unfriendly, the family as a concept is being put to the test. The traditional image of the nuclear family, consisting of parents and children, is expanding. New family forms and cohabitations are emerging that replace, complement or replicate classic extended family structures.

The way we live as a family today inevitably shapes future generations. In an increasingly individualized world, intergenerational relationships are invaluable. Today, young and old often live spatially and emotionally separated from each other in everyday life. This not only shapes our individual courses of life but has an impact on the professional world and society. If there are no intergenerational relationships in the family, generational conflicts in the professional context and society are inevitable. Togetherness must be organized much more consciously and promoted at an early stage because that will be an important key in the future to be able to overcome crises together.

Against this background, the question is no less than how we want to live together as a society in the future. The answer to this is fundamental to formulating political programs that truly understand and support the needs of families. It is not only about reliable state services but about shaping a culture that promotes and values coexistence across generations. The question of the future of the family thus revolves not only around its role as a social safety net but also about shaping the coexistence of the generations. How we as a society shape these relationships, what support we offer to families, and how we harness the potential of all generations will not only influence the well-being of individuals but also determine how resilient and viable our society as a whole will be.

The future of the family is therefore not only a private or a political question, but a cultural challenge that affects us all. How we make decisions today and what priorities we set will have a significant impact on the way we live tomorrow.

More information about the author via the QR code:
www.familyvalued.org/Ana-Hoffmeister-2

Prof. Dr. Ulrich Reinhardt

Trend Researcher
Germany

The Renaissance of the Family

Abstract

Even though the family is the most important thing for German citizens, birth rates remain low. In eight out of ten areas, there is less consensus on reasons against starting a family than there was in 2014! The compatibility of family and career, especially for women, is not considered sufficient. This is partly due to care work being seen mainly as a woman's task. Another factor is the uncertainty about the future. The prognosis is nevertheless positive. The gradual decrease in concerns about having children clearly shows that it is quite possible to actively influence the birth rate.

Article

Family is and remains the most important thing, a large majority of Germans agree with this statement. Due to the lockdowns and restrictions during the Corona pandemic and the resulting forced closeness to the family, more and more Germans actually feel more connected to their families. One in two citizens even says that they have (re)discovered the value of the family. Contrary to widespread opinion, the family is not an obsolete model. On the contrary, a renaissance of the family is being clearly heralded because – especially in uncertain times – one's own family proves to be a reliable anchor and the most important thing in the lives of many citizens.

Nevertheless, the birth rate in Germany is low at 1.46 children per woman, because many couples are currently consciously deciding against having children of their own. The reasons for this are manifold and range from financial burdens to a lack of state support, to the fear of divorce and of single parenting. In a 10-year comparison, however, fears are decreasing. In eight out of ten areas, there is less consensus on reasons against starting a family than there was in 2014!

The two main reasons cited by Germans against starting a family are the high financial burden and the difficulties in reconciling work and family life. Despite efforts by companies to offer more family-friendly structures, the compatibility of family and career remains a challenge for many parents. Implementation is still not easy, especially for women. Only about one in four citizens expects better compatibility between job and family for women over the coming years.

There are various reasons for this rather sceptical attitude. One of the main reasons lies in the still firmly anchored traditional expectations within society, according to which care work is mainly to be done by women. Women themselves tend to exclude themselves from certain professions due to gender stereotypes, and women interrupt their careers for the sake of the family much more often than men. This is due, among other things, to their generally lower income and consequently to concerns about greater financial losses if the father takes paternity leave. In addition, women are more often exposed to the double burden of both professional and family responsibilities without adequate support and working conditions (e.g. guaranteed childcare places or flexible working hours).

As another central reason against having their own children Germans cite the general uncertainty regarding the future. This is the only area where concern has increased (see below). Almost half of Germans are now worried about future social developments, whether in terms of economic growth, climate change or conflicts. Putting a child into this world therefore seems irresponsible for many couples.

Outlook

Gradually decreasing concerns about having children clearly show that it is quite possible to actively influence the birth rate. The right framework conditions can remove the fears and burdens of potential parents. In the future, politicians will continue to

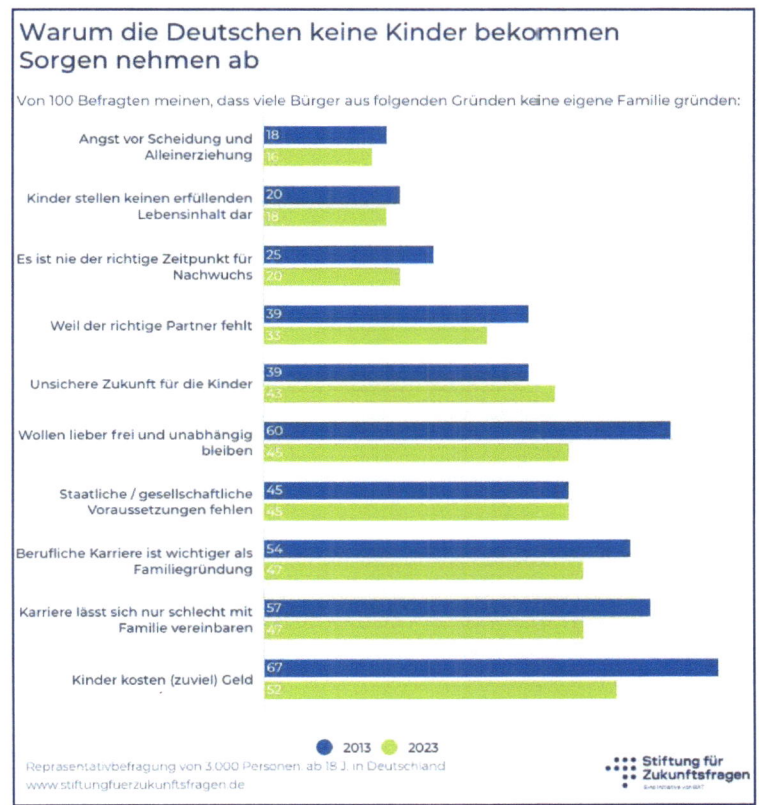

Warum die Deutschen keine Kinder bekommen
Sorgen nehmen ab

Von 100 Befragten meinen, dass viele Bürger aus folgenden Gründen keine eigene Familie gründen:

Grund	2013	2023
Angst vor Scheidung und Alleinerziehung	18	16
Kinder stellen keinen erfüllenden Lebensinhalt dar	20	18
Es ist nie der richtige Zeitpunkt für Nachwuchs	25	20
Weil der richtige Partner fehlt	39	33
Unsichere Zukunft für die Kinder	39	43
Wollen lieber frei und unabhängig bleiben	60	45
Staatliche / gesellschaftliche Voraussetzungen fehlen	45	45
Berufliche Karriere ist wichtiger als Familiegründung	54	47
Karriere lässt sich nur schlecht mit Familie vereinbaren	57	47
Kinder kosten (zuviel) Geld	67	52

● 2013   ● 2023

Repräsentativbefragung von 3.000 Personen ab 18 J. in Deutschland
www.stiftungfuerzukunftsfragen.de

Stiftung für Zukunftsfragen

be called upon to improve these framework conditions for families. The federal government currently cites over 150 different family benefits.

Of these around 48 billion euros are provided annually for child benefit alone. In addition, companies will in future have to better promote the compatibility of family and career – whether through more flexible working time models or a more supportive corporate culture – in order to be attractive to both parents in the long term. Ultimately the decision to have their own family lies with each citizen and will continue to do so in the future. And despite all the fears, compromises and restrictions, people are increasingly recognizing how much children can contribute to increasing the quality of life and personal happiness.

More information about the author via the QR code:
http://www.familyvalued.org/Ulrich-Reinhardt-2

Madeleine Wallin

Entrepreneur
FEFAF General Secretary
Permanent Representative UN-NY
Sweden

Rediscovering the Value of Motherhood

Abstract

Mothers are the main protectors of life and deserve the highest recognition for taking this responsibility. Well-being is typically measured in GDP, and everything revolves around economics and growth; whereas reproduction and that which creates, nurtures and protects all living things, is given little or no value. Caring for other people is the very opposite of destruction.

Article

Becoming a mother is transformative, and there is a life before and after. It is a transformation that should be given more space and the starring role it deserves. One goes from being an independent, free individual to a life where you almost consist of two people: first during pregnancy when your body is the child's home, and then as the primary caregiver where someone else's needs must come first. It is challenging and comes naturally to some women, while others feel overwhelmed, perhaps due to previous experience. The "transformation" from woman to mother is a time when women deserve support and recognition.

Women are the vessels, the mothers - those who give life. Not all women become mothers, some because they can't, some because they don't want to. A woman's fertile age usually begins between the ages of 13 and 18 and lasts approximately until the age of 50. Postponing childbearing can create difficulties as she is most

15

fertile between the ages of 20-25. From the age of 35, it drops quickly until meno-pause, when the ability to conceive disappears. The woman's biological clock should have a higher status as a clear guide for women and society.

There should be a time in life that is protected and reserved for women to have children without undue stress. The ability to create new life is crucial to humanity. That a human being is formed and lives in a woman's body is amazing - a creation story so fascinating that it is difficult to find anything greater. Why then is reproduction and the care of children still not the most highly valued matter in all humanity?

Caring for other people is the very opposite of destruction. Despite all the negative consequences that wars and environmental destruction bring, they still count as economic factors, whereas looking after and caring for those closest to you does not. Economic value is considered to be created only when someone performs a service for money. To make the care count as an economic factor we outsource unpaid care work and thus force separations between children and mothers. If another mother takes care of my child, it counts in the economy, if I do it myself, it is economically invisible. The question is, do both produce the same outcome?

"Mothers are the main protectors of life and deserve the highest recognition for taking this responsibility"

Well-being is measured in GDP, and everything revolves around economy and growth, whereas reproduction and that which creates, nurtures and protects all living things, is given little or no value.

Care is the very essence of life. Most people intuit this, but for many the realization comes only at the very end. What really counted in my life? Wasn't it my relationships - the love I received and the love I gave?

Motherhood, or mothering, is a cure or antidote to egotism, power and destruction: thus, the importance of care relationships needs to be recognized. The attachment between the child and the primary caregiver, most often the mother, is crucial when brain develops at rapid speed with more than 1 million neural connections every second during the first years. This is the time when the foundations for future learning, behaviour, and health are formed. For bonding to occur one needs to be present. And I dare to say that the mother is the most important. She can be replaced but, for the child, the natural mother must be the first choice, as they already have the strongest bond from the time when her body was its world. Another reason is that each mother's breast milk is unique and adapted precisely to her child.

Care is the heart of society, and it is time to value and recognize that fact, for instance by using more nuanced metrics than mere GDP. Financial security must be strengthened throughout the life cycle, the rights of unpaid caregivers upheld, and their voices considered in political decision-making. Article 25:2 of the UN Human Rights Act states that "Motherhood and childhood are entitled to special care and assistance" and there are strong reasons to take these words seriously.

Mothers are the main protectors of life and deserve the highest recognition for taking this responsibility.

More information about the author via the QR code:
www.familyvalued.org/Madeleine-Wallin-2

Prof. Brad Wilcox

Professor of Sociology and
Director of the
National Marriage Project
University of Virginia
United States of America

Marriage Matters More Than Ever

Abstract

Our culture is increasingly sending us the message that money, work, and freedom from family are the recipe for a prosperous and happy life today. I call this the "Midas Mindset." Many left-leaning mainstream organs of opinion make this argument with women in mind.

Meanwhile, on the right, prominent online influencers like Pearl Davis and Andrew Tate are also pushing the Midas Mindset—but with a focus on men. They argue marriage is a bad deal for guys.

Messaging like this helps explain why today more Americans think education, work and money are more "important" for fulfilment than marriage and why the marriage rate has fallen 60% in the last fifty years.

Article

Mammon or Marriage?

Our culture is increasingly sending us the message that money, work, and freedom from family are the recipe for a prosperous and happy life today. I call this the "Midas Mindset." Many left-leaning mainstream organs of opinion make this argument with women in mind. One prominent financial outlet ran with this headline: "Women Who Stay Single and Don't Have Kids are Getting Richer." Another big outlet offered "The Case Against Marriage."

"That's because nothing predicts happiness in America like a good mar-riage"

Meanwhile, on the right, prominent online influencers like Pearl Davis and Andrew Tate are also pushing the Midas Mindset—but with a focus on men. They argue marriage is a bad deal for guys. In Tate's words: "The problem is, there is zero advantage to marriage in the Western world for a man" – especially because "it's very common that women" divorce their husbands. So, any man in his right mind ought to stay single, make lots of money, and use—but not invest in—the opposite sex.

Messaging like this helps explain why today more Americans think education, work and money are more "important" for fulfilment than marriage and why the marriage rate has fallen 60% in the last fifty years.

But this message about marriage and family could not be more wrong. That's because nothing predicts happiness in America like a good marriage, not education, work, money, not even sex. The data tells us that men and women who are in a good marriage are 545% more likely to be very happy with their lives compared to their fellow Americans who are unmarried or in unhappy marriages. What's more: No group of American men AND women (18-55) are happier than those who are married mothers and fathers. So, in the real world, marriage matters more than Mammon when it comes to endowing our lives with meaning, purpose, and happiness.

"But, of course, marriage is not just about happiness."

Why Marriage Matters

Why does marriage matter so much? We are, as Aristotle taught, social animals. We are hardwired to connect. That's why our ties with others— family and friends—end up being so much more crucial to our welfare than things like the size of our bank account or the degree on our wall. And because for most of us no relationship is as important as our marriage, that's why nothing compares to a good relationship when it comes to giving us a shot at being happy—most of the time.

But, of course, marriage is not just about happiness. Marriage is also about money, it's about meaning, it's about being less likely to feel alone. We know, for instance, that men and women who get and stay married earn more and save more. This is why married men and women have about 10 times the assets of their peers who are single in their 50s. And they are significantly less likely to be poor across the course of their lives.

Married men and women with children also report much more meaning and significantly less loneliness than their peers who are single and childless. They are over 50% more likely to report that their lives are meaningful, for instance.

"Of course, there are also happy singles and unhappy spouses."

Consider one thirtysomething man from the outer suburbs of Washington D.C. who I call Scott. By the standards of success in today's culture, nothing should bother Scott, 34, who is unmarried. He's got a college degree from Clemson University, an engaging career as a military contractor, a house of his own, and a six-figure salary. But these educational and professional accomplishments are not enough. "You know, I've got degrees on my wall, I've got accomplishments and certificates, but it doesn't mean anything in the end," he told me. Scott feels alone and at sea on many a day. "I have to get up every day and look in the mirror and realize I'm alone. I have nobody." Not surprisingly, Scott is struggling with a toxic mix of loneliness, meaninglessness, and Sadness.

Of course, all of us know single people who are thriving and married men and women who are struggling. But, on average, the meaning, direction, and sense of solidarity supplied by marriage is invaluable to ordinary men and women.

Is Marriage a Bad Bet?
Many Americans worry that marriage is a bad bet, partly because they think 1-in-2 marriages end in divorce. But that statistic is no longer true. The divorce rate has fallen 40% since 1980, which means that most marriages go the distance today. This also means that most kids born to married parents today will be raised in a stably married home. In other words, the clear majority of Americans who marry today are managing to make it.

And it's not just that they are stably married, they are happily married. Today, 62% of husbands and wives say they are "very" happy in their marriages and an extra 34% say they are "pretty happy" in their marriages. Of course, most couples

have ups and downs, days, weeks, months, and even years when marriage and life are tough. But, on average, most of the time, American husbands and wives report they are happily married.

I identify four groups of Americans who are "masters of marriage"—Asian, religious, college-educated and conservative Americans—who are especially likely to be forging strong and stable marriages today. Asian, religious, and college-educated couples lead out in marital stability. Religious, college-educated, and conservative Americans top the charts in marital happiness. So, marriage is an especially good bet for these groups. I explain why in the book.

Defy the Elites, Forge a Strong Family

One reason today's masters of marriage are more likely to succeed at marriage is that they reject many of the messages coming from the elites who control the commanding heights of our culture. Too often today, journalists, professors, Hollywood types, and other professionals stress a "me-first" approach to love and marriage that privileges autonomy, freedom, and self-interest. Articles in mainstream publications celebrate extramarital sexual choices, financial gurus talk up separate checking accounts, and celebrated therapists encourage men and women to prioritize number one in their marriages.

But this me-first approach to marriage is a dead end in the real world. That's because couples who adapt a "we-before-me" approach to marriage and embrace time-tested virtues like commitment and fidelity are much more likely to flourish in their marriages. The data tell us, for instance, that couples who hold to the classic ideal that infidelity is "always wrong," who share their money in joint accounts, and who embrace an ethic of marital generosity are markedly happier in their marriages. They also seem less likely to land in divorce court.

So, to build on the subtitle of my book, I say, defy the elites and forge a strong family by taking a "we-before-me" approach to marriage and family life.

"The benefits associated with raising children in an intact family have grown recently."

For the sake of the kids and the country?

"*Isn't divorce less of a big deal for kids these days?*" A colleague's wife asked me this question during a break from an academic conference. "After all," she added, "we're more accepting now of all sorts of families." Her theory was this: because kids in nontraditional families are less likely to feel ostracized or stigmatized nowadays, they are as well less likely to be harmed by family breakdown than they would have been a half-century ago. This view is increasingly common. Many people think marriage and a stable family are less important for children and adults in the contemporary world than they once were.

But this view could not be more wrong. In fact, for many outcomes, the advantages associated with being raised in an intact family have actually grown recently. For instance, the connection between family structure and school suspensions as well as college graduations has grown tighter recently. More generally, kids raised in intact, married families are significantly more likely to be thriving financially, socially, and emotionally. Probably the most striking finding regarding kids in Get Married is that young men raised in any kind of non-intact family—from a single-parent to a stepfamily—are more likely to have spent some time in jail or prison than to have graduated from college. This is very much the opposite for young men who grew up with their own married parents.

And when you look at poor kids' odds of realizing the American Dream—going from rags to riches over the course of their lives—what you see is that the #1 factor predicting this kind of mobility at the community level is the share of two-parent families in a community. This is but one of the findings that tells us that strong and stable families matter not just for individual kids but for the country as a whole.

To be sure, many kids raised outside an intact, married home turn out fine. I was raised by a single mom and am doing fine. But as a sociologist I can tell you that, on average, kids and communities are more likely to thrive when they are rooted in strong, married families. This is why, if you wish to "save civilization" you should care about the health of our most important social institution, marriage.

More information about the author via the QR code:

www.familyvalued.org/Brad-Wilcox-2

Hermann Binkert

Founder and Managing Partner
of the INSA-CONSULERE GmbH
Germany

The traditional family is the model for the future

Abstract

Those who are passionate about strengthening the family often have the feeling that they are fighting a hopeless battle. And indeed, most headlines give the impression that the traditional family is outdated.

The family situation as experienced by oneself, the statistical data on the situation of families in Germany, and how family feels for the individual are three different realities, each of which must be taken seriously in its own right. INSA explored the subjective family experience in a large family study in Spring 2022.

Article

Those who are passionate about strengthening the family often have the feeling that they are fighting a hopeless battle. And indeed, most headlines give the impression that the traditional family is outdated. The concept of family is also increasingly being widened: thus, some nowadays would define a family as at least two generations using the same refrigerator!

Around 70 percent of all family households in Germany are so-called traditional family households with mother, father and child(ren). And the acceptance of the "traditional family" in the population as a whole is also high: 61 percent of the respondents we surveyed representatively in the INSA opinion poll associate something positive with the "traditional family", 30 percent something neither positive nor

negative, and only one in twenty (5 percent) with something negative. Among respondents with children, as many as 70 percent see something positive in the "traditional family".

"More than two-thirds of all respondents would be most likely to turn to their own family in a crisis."

The family situation experienced by oneself, the statistical data on the situation of families in Germany, and how family feels for the individual are three different realities, each of which must be taken seriously in its own right. INSA explored the subjective family experience in a large family study in Spring 2022.

Our family study has clearly shown, among other things, that contentedness and personal happiness are influenced not only by income, age and state of health, but also by the respondents' attitude to the family: Those who have started a family, or are planning to do so, are more likely to be happy (70 to 58 percent) and contented (77 to 62 percent) than those respondents who do not plan to start their own family. These family-friendly persons are also less likely to feel lonely (23 to 30 percent) and less likely to have, or to have had, depression (24 to 33 percent), which in turn fits in with the perception that the family offers security and protection for many in our crisis-ridden times: More than two-thirds of all respondents (68 percent) would be most likely to turn to their own family in a crisis.

"For 80 percent, it is important to be a member of a family themselves."

The fact that the "traditional family" is the most widespread form of family, and that family is generally rated very positively, does not change the prevailing tolerance towards those who decide against the traditional family model of father, mother and child(ren): Not even one in four (23 percent) of those we surveyed in the family study finds a decision against the traditional family model bad. Most respondents simply didn't care if others decided against the traditional family model (42 percent).

However, this tolerance does not diminish the special esteem for families. For example, a clear majority (58 percent) thinks that people who have started their own family are seen more positively by society than people who have not. Also, 70 percent of all respondents see family households as more capable of tasks or responsibilities to than single households, and for 80 percent it is important to be a member of a family themselves.

Whether it is about work, freedom, quality of life, social orientation or security – the family always has a clear predominantly positive influence, and this positive influence is still more pronounced among respondents who are planning to start a family or have already started a family. Twice as many respondents say about their lives that they have spent too little time with their families (22 percent) than say the same about their professions (11 percent).

As important as the family is to Germans, they are dissatisfied with government family policies, according to a recent survey in the INSA opinion trend: Only one in three (34 percent) thinks that the interests of families are currently sufficiently considered in German politics. The majority (53 percent), on the other hand, deny this. Almost three-quarters of the respondents we surveyed (72 percent) are also in favour of remuneration of family duties, i.e. that the care and nursing of family members be subsidized by the state, for example with a salary for child-raising.

Personally, I see a deficit in the appreciation of families – and that does not just mean financial support. In my opinion, what is needed is a child-friendly climate in society and an orientation towards the best interests of the child.

It is often overlooked that family upbringing has a great influence on the further development of young people. The quality of the relationship between parents and children is decisive for their later ability to bond, which in turn is an important prerequisite for learning ability.

There is much to be said for Hans-Werner Sinn's analysis that "the few young people who will still exist despite child poverty" will "remember traditional ways of life and, shaking their heads, will reject a life model that instead leaves the old impoverished due to lack of family support".

It seems to me that an intellectual offensive in favour of the family is needed. Family must be seen not only from a functional point of view. It has a fundamental role to play in the state and society. Only a strong family, as the smallest unit of a subsidiary order, is a good foundation for a successful society. In my opinion, the majority of the population is ahead of politics with this insight.

More information about the author via the QR code:

www.familyvalued.org/Hermann-Binkert-2

Susanne Hartfiel
Social scientist & author
Germany

The Forgotten Potential of the Family

Abstract

Families can integrate various people, such as sick or disabled members and people of all ages. But families in the Western world are in crisis. They hardly have any time left for family work and unpaid community-building commitments. All-day daycare centres and schools and inpatient care and facilities for the disabled provide relief for the nuclear family by ostracizing the weaker family members. Society is also fragmented into countless groups, which sometimes have little to do with each other. This does not have to be the case. The article describes ways in which interested families, individuals and groups can organize together to develop ways of life in which weaker family members are part of the community. The state is not released from its responsibility. However, in the spirit of the principle of subsidiarity, it should support families where they lack the opportunities and offer people professional help where they live.

Article

Families can integrate a variety of different people, such as sick and disabled members as well as people of all ages **Families are the basic unit of society.** They exist before the state and members of well-functioning families continue to support each other even when state institutions no longer function. But **families in the Western world are in crisis**. There are numerous reasons for this, such as the

alternative forms of living together that have been propagated for decades and are now also politically promoted, the high mobility, the low birth rate, and the full-time employment of many people. Family members often live far apart. Fewer and fewer young people have to support an ever-increasing number of old people, while the employment of usually both parents often leave little time for family work and social commitment.

"Today's nuclear families are often overwhelmed."

Even in the 20th century, large families existed all over the Western world, whose members lived together in a spatially manageable area and enabled children to grow up not only with their parents, but also with numerous siblings, cousins, (great-) aunts and uncles, (great-) grandparents, and all their friends and acquaintances. There were only a few single parents. Even in the 1970s, larger groups of children played freely on the streets in the afternoons, even in the big cities, while the adults of the neighbourhood kept an eye on them. Old people were less likely to be alone. Often there was someone from the family unit or the neighbourhood nearby who could keep company and give small help.

"Life in large families was not an idyll, but especially for old and disabled people, it was often better than their current life as home residents."

Today's **nuclear families are often overwhelmed.** Both parents work together outside the home for considerably longer than the sole earner of previous families. Their everyday life is punctuated by gainful employment, appointments and chauffeur services for their children, whose daycare centres, schools and leisure activities are often no longer nearby. If illness or other unpredictable events disrupt the schedule, considerable organizational effort must be spent. Old people usually live on their own and move to a nursing home towards the end of their lives. People die in hospitals and care facilities, only rarely at home. The state and state-funded independent agencies have created **facilities** for all age groups **to relieve the stressed families by outsourcing their weakest members and to enable the full-time**

employment of the most productive, as desired by employers: all-day daycare centres and schools, facilities for the disabled, and nursing homes. Children, the disabled and the elderly are cared for there by overworked, often underpaid staff, suffering from staff shortages and excessive bureaucracy, who cannot do justice to the individuals in their care, even with a lot of goodwill and commitment, among them many migrants who have left their relatives behind in their country of origin.

Life in the extended family was never idyllic, but especially for old and disabled people it was often better than their current lives as care-home residents. If you talk to people who have lived in such institutions for a long time, you hear about their **longing for family, friendship and relationships**. Their everyday life is dominated by professionals. There are few, sometimes no more, unpaid relationships at all in their lives. All the People they deal with every day are paid for it. This is injurious because there is no such thing as paid friendship. Some care homes are really death centres. The caregivers are responsible for such a large number of residents that poor care, inadequate medical care, neglect and actual avoidable mistakes are the order of the day. In this way, a negative health domino effect is easily triggered, which quickly leads to the death of the already vulnerable people. The increasing social acceptance of assisted suicide and euthanasia too is related to this desolate supply situation.

There are also alternative models in the Western world for dealing with such situations. This includes **communities that actively integrate vulnerable people**. One example is the Catholic Worker communities that originally emerged in New York City. They consist of families, small groups and individuals who live close to each other and have a common concern, such as the provision of housing and support for the homeless. The individual families and groups offer support to a limited number of people and support each other and their family members. One family with a large house, for example, takes in a homeless person who becomes part of the family and is involved in the work in the house according to his abilities. Another family has adopted two disabled children. Another family takes care of the seriously ill grandfather who lives in the house.

A large family has equipped one floor of their house with guest rooms for the homeless, so that they can stay with them temporarily in an emergency. Every evening the family members, their guests and helpers gather around a large table for dinner. Another group has set itself the goal of offering a meal for rich and poor in a friendly

atmosphere twice a week. Socially privileged people serve poor and homeless people, eat together with them and get to know and appreciate each other in this way. All families and groups are supported by volunteers who cook food, look after children, do repair work or shopping, or keep a grandfather company when he cannot be left alone. Sometimes young people live with a family for a few months and receive board and lodging in exchange for agreed help activities. The different Catholic Worker communities are very heterogeneous.

What is done, how, why and for whom depends heavily on the parties involved. What they have in common is the concern to overcome the discrepancy between the privileged and the less privileged, between the poor and the rich, through houses of hospitality and community life. They do this without state support and live off their own work and/or donations made to them by individuals. Some also use professional services, such as outpatient care services to support the care of their old and sick family members or a professional detoxification program for relapsed alcoholics. In doing so, they are careful not to grant undue control over their family members to social institutions or government agencies. Often, the communities are supported by professionals who provide their services free of charge. For example, a dentist produces free dentures for poor people, a journalist publishes an appeal for donations, a lawyer provides his legal expertise, or a supermarket owner delivers food free of charge.

Families who practice home schooling are organized in a similar way to the Catholic Worker communities: In countries where school attendance is not compulsory, parents have the opportunity to educate their children themselves. They often do this in community with other families living nearby.

As in a normal school, small or larger groups of students are taught by different adults in this way. In the afternoons, sports and leisure activities are offered to the students. Their joint program also includes cultural activities and services for the elderly, sick or disadvantaged, whether individually or collectively. Each family has its own house, yet the families live together. People support each other, celebrate joint festivals and are happy about the good development of the children and young people, who do not grow up as spoiled only-children, but learn skills from a large number of different people that would be more difficult to teach in a nuclear family and age-homogeneous groups of students. Negative social influences such as early sexualisation, drug abuse, excessive media use and the like are easier to control because children grow up in communal relationships that involve them in meaningful activities and give them a positive foundation of values before they are confronted with the corresponding social aberrations.

The Protestant Bruderhof communities, which emerged in Germany in the 1920s and emigrated to England, Paraguay and later also North America and Australia because of their persecution by the National Socialists, also live together as larger or smaller family groups. Single people are also welcome in their communities.

Some communities have up to 300 members and fill an entire village, others are more like large house communities. They share their lives, practice agriculture, own their own companies and have members who are trained and active in various craft or academic professions. Interested young people can live and work with them for a while.

The Community considers all work for and within the Community to be of equal value. If, for example, a large family needs support, it receives it from other, often young, still unmarried community members. In the same way, old, sick and disabled people are cared for at home in their own homes. The care of a person suffering from dementia, for example, is therefore equivalent to other activities, such as agricultural or manual work or the activities of a doctor or company boss. Since Bruderhof members share their property, everyone can be provided with everything they need to live.

The era of large families is certainly over and can hardly be revived today in society as a whole. However, the communities described above show that with a little creativity, it is possible to create networks and communities that allow families with children and/or elderly, sick or disabled relatives to live a life with their weaker members. In many Western countries, disabled people today have a legal right to participate in the life of society. How this is implemented is another matter. There is often a lack of conceptual and practical support for those who are tasked with realizing this participation, such as teachers at general education schools. Integration is possible when people can meet each other positively in everyday life and the context of normal activities, discover common ground and identify with each other. Anyone who wants integration must therefore create framework conditions that enable and promote such positive encounters and mutual identification processes. When people identify

with others, they want to spend time with them, please them, and be similar to them in certain important aspects. They wish them well and speak well of them. They are willing to take responsibility for them. It is beyond the scope of this article to elaborate on the numerous aspects that such identification and integration processes promote.

It is important to note that a well-functioning family is naturally integrative, because if children in their family learn to live cooperatively with people of different ages, to support weak, sick and disabled relatives or friends in everyday life and to value everyone equally, then they will later be able to transfer these attitudes and skills to other areas of society. If children learn that all people have something to contribute, then they will later expect this contribution from those people who initially seem strange to them. From this perspective, it makes little sense to question the natural family, to weaken it politically or to outsource its functions to the state and welfare associations while at the same time to propagating inclusion and diversity. Such a policy is in reality a permanent job creation measure for members of social and care professions: they manage exclusion in order to (re-)integrate the excluded later. It would be better to actively strengthen and support families and their naturally integrative function.

An important aspect of the communities and family networks described above is their willingness to engage with other people free of charge and to contribute financially to the community according to their respective abilities. This is not completely uncommon elsewhere in the Western world either, because in fact many people are willing to take on voluntary work or donate to a good cause. However, this voluntary commitment is often aimed at an institution or is institutionally mediated. You donate to a charitable organization instead of directly to a poor family. You volunteer to help out in a facility for the disabled instead of inviting a disabled resident to your home. You do a voluntary social year instead of temporarily becoming part of a community or community organized family.

The two types: donation and free help are fundamentally different in their approach: The institutionally provided or mediated help always follows the rules of the institution, i.e. the charitable institution with all its dysfunctionalities, which professional institutions always have (e.g. due to legal requirements, bureaucratic processes, etc.), regardless of the individual personal commitment of their employees.

Individual personal encounters between supporters and supporters are often more difficult here, among other things because the encounters within the facilities usually take place with groups of disadvantaged people instead of with individuals or families. Supporters donate their time or money, but don't actually share their lives.

Donations for charitable purposes or voluntary work within social institutions can be useful, but should never replace real personal encounters and support, because without a personal relationship, no community of any kind is possible. Without a personal relationship, no real understanding of the life situation and perspective of disadvantaged people can develop. Anyone who wants integration or inclusion should therefore ask whether they themselves maintain positive personal and unpaid relationships with people who are socially disadvantaged due to age, illness, disability or other reasons and how these relationships could be improved and intensified.

Another common feature of the communities described above is the appreciation of unpaid work. This voluntary, community-serving work is supported by those who earn money through their professional work. In this way, family and educational work, the schooling of children and the support and care of people in need become possible. Many old and disabled people do not need 24-hour care, as offered by the professional help system. It is often enough for other people to live in are present and responsive in their living or working environment. Young people today are often told that a career is the best way to a fulfilled life. Universities are bursting at the seams, filled with young people who hope to find their dream job later on, but also with those who have little interest in their field of study or intellectual work, but think they need the degree to be able to live well. They all live a kind of extended youth, postpone starting a family until later and sometimes waste time that they would need to build up their independent life and acquire the necessary professional and human skills. Some are in debt after graduation and are therefore not completely free to shape their lives. The dream job is only available to a few and work alone rarely conveys fulfilment or meaning in life. Well-functioning families and communities often have a more balanced relationship with paid work. They use it to finance their communal life. Their identity is not only determined by professional work and career, but just as much by family and community relationships and activities.

Another principle of well-functioning communities and family networks is the active participation of all members. Everyone has their place, their obligations, everyone

makes their contribution, no matter how small they may seem. Sometimes it turns out that those who seem weak possess something that the people who know them well enough feel is a great gift for their lives. Good communities are characterized by recognizing the gift of individual members and looking for ways to make it accessible to the community. Because community thrives on exchange. It does not work if some members are only the givers and doers and others are only the passive receivers. Of course, responsibilities and tasks are distributed quite differently. What is important is a core of stable members who have committed themselves to supporting the community or family network and living in it permanently and who certainly bear more responsibility than those who only participate temporarily. Nevertheless, everyone's contribution to the common whole is important.

Ideally, communities and family networks are also united by a common worldview from which community-promoting values and actions can be derived. While people of other worldviews can participate or be recipients of support and solidarity, there should be consensus among senior members about the common worldview and shared values. This is not the same as belonging to a religious community or NGO. Although community members can be recruited from church congregations, religious communities or associations, they should not be founded and managed by their employees or representatives. Especially in countries like Germany, where churches financed by church tax, the state, state-funded welfare associations and NGOs have covered all areas of life with their structures, guidelines and rules, it seems important that families and communities reclaim at least part of their autonomy. Many state, social and church institutions are functioning less and less. It is time for people and families to reflect on their very own concerns and tasks and to take action themselves instead of placing their hopes in these institutions.

Nevertheless, the state and churches are not relieved of their responsibility. In the spirit of the principle of subsidiarity, they should support families where the families lack opportunities, and they should offer professional help to people where they live. This includes a family and economic policy that allows time for family work. Families, for example, should be enabled to live at least modestly on a single income at times. How the gainful employment is then divided within the family would be up to the family itself. Whether time for family work would be best realized through higher minimum wages, tax relief, cash transfers to large families, or a combination of such and similar measures, would have to be discussed.

It would also be important to build social housing that provides sufficient affordable accommodation for large families or, alternatively, generous subsidies for the purchase of property. A deficit in the area of residential construction also lies in the often very uniform apartment sizes in many urban apartment buildings. It would be important to have a spectrum of all apartment sizes in the same building in order to enable spatial coexistence in different family or community constellations.

In many Western countries, there is also an urgent need to expand outpatient services for the elderly and disabled at the expense of the ever-growing in-patient facilities, so that these people can be cared for and supported at home in their homes, within or near their families and friends. Bureaucratic and structural hurdles in the use of outpatient services would also have to be removed. Many professional services could also be designed to be many more needs based. For example, people in need of care in Germany are entitled to benefits from long-term care insurance, but those in need of care and their families are massively disadvantaged compared to professional providers. If a professional service organizes and provides the care service, it receives almost twice as much remuneration as the family that does it itself. At the same time, professional care services are often not in a position to provide care reliably, at the agreed time and in appropriate quality. Sometimes they delegate the coordination of their caregivers to the relatives. Other services that older people typically need (such as help with household chores, shopping or administrative activities, accompaniment to doctor's appointments or other activities outside the home) are severely underfunded and are also provided by other providers.

Many families are hopelessly overwhelmed with the coordination and bureaucratic administration of these different services and responsibilities, which is a decisive reason why so many families see no alternative to a nursing home when their relatives are increasingly in need of care and support. In the area of services for disabled people, at least in some large cities, there are assistance services where all the services that a person needs are provided by the same provider. The assistance user has personal assistants at his disposal who do everything that the person in question needs, whether it is personal hygiene, household support, participation in social life or anything else. Here, too, the coordination of assistants is often difficult, and the

quality of care and support is often significantly deficient, as in the field of services for the elderly. At the very least, however, the lives of assistance users are not fragmented by different responsibilities and providers, as is the case with old people.

Well-functioning families, family networks and communities can compensate for some things that do not work or work poorly with professional providers. Its members can step in if the daycare centre closes earlier due to a lack of staff, or the nursing service is unreliable. You can check whether agreed professional services are actually provided or offered in the agreed quality and act accordingly should this not be the case. They can use their own contacts and networks to get important information or support for their loved ones. Many options in our lives, such as a new job, new leisure activities or new friendships, are informally mediated by family members, friends or acquaintances. Children, the elderly and disabled people who are part of a well-functioning family or community automatically share in these contacts and relationships and the resulting opportunities. Sometimes they need support in taking advantage of such opportunities. This type of support can also be offered by families or communities.

It is high time to counter the general social fragmentation into seemingly homogeneous groups, in which extensive special offers for all age groups, life situations and worldviews are the rule and people live predominantly in isolation with their own kind or as less capable people. This social model of fragmentation would have to be countered by community models that bring together people's abilities and weaknesses and unite them into a complementary whole. Because diversity is not only a challenge but can also lead to something new and beautiful through mutual complementarity. The family is the natural place to start such a defragmentation, because it is naturally inclusive, i.e. a place for everyone. However, the prerequisite for activating this potential of the family is a look beyond the horizon of one's own nuclear family or individualistic way of life-to-life plans that enable community and neighbourliness. With creativity, personal commitment and a realistic view of what the state and welfare associations can and cannot achieve, a lot is possible.

More information about the author via the QR code:
www.familyvalued.org/Susanne-Hartfiel-2

Prof. Matteo Rizzolli

Univ. LUMSA

Italy

The reason for government family policy

Abstract

Our basic thesis is that a society based mainly on intact families is more efficient than a society based on individuals, especially if those intact families are founded on marriage. Family efficiency has various aspects that are empirically measurable, and all related to individual and social well-being. Before I go any further, I would like to point out once again that economic efficiency should not be the only possible criterion for family policy; there is at least one more that deals with the question of justice.

Article

The family increases the physical and mental health of the individual

There is extensive and solid literature that includes the medical, epidemiological, psychological sciences, as well as demography and sociology, and has examined the relationship between family status and various objective measures of well-being, such as life expectancy and health. Many studies have linked higher mortality for singles, separated/divorced and widowers than for married/cohabiting people (Ikeda et al., 2007; Manzoli et al., 2007; Molloy et al., 2009; Sbarra et al., 2011). Specific medical studies have found that married people have a better prognosis in the event of a heart attack (Dupre & Nelson, 2016) and a higher probability of surviving cancer (Kravdal, 2001). A study conducted in Denmark that followed 6.5 million Danes between 1982 and 2011 found that same-sex marriages consistently led to lower

mortality rates than those of other categories of marital status (Frisch & Simonsen, 2013). Similarly for the USA, Rendall et al. (2011) found a higher life expectancy for married couples, in this case using large-scale panel data, and highlighted that marriage is particularly beneficial for the survival of men.

With regard to mental health, an impressive number of studies have also found a robust positive association between marital status and mental health (Gove et al., 1983, 1990; Pearlin & Johnson, 1977; Ross & Mirowsky, 1989); marriage, for example, has been shown to be a protective factor against suicide risk (Masocco et al., 2008).

The implications for public policy are obvious, as health is one of the main items of expenditure in modern welfare systems. This literature suggests, on the one hand, that neglecting the health of families affects the health of individuals, and on the other hand, it suggests that family policy and health policy are partly interchangeable. In summary: More families, more health!

The family increases the happiness and satisfaction of the individual

In addition to physical and mental health, which can be measured with objective variables, there is extensive literature that examines the influence of family structure and relationships on subjective well-being, such as happiness and life satisfaction. The relationship between marriage and happiness is one of the earliest and most robust findings in this literature (Glenn, 1975; Wood et al., 1989), and this result has proven to be robust both in international comparisons, showing that the association between marital status and subjective well-being is similarly positive in different cultures (Diener et al., 2000; Mastekaasa, 1994) and their temporal stability: Despite a phenomenon known in the literature as hedonic adaptation, empirical evidence suggests that while initial enthusiasm may wane over time, overall happiness and satisfaction may remain stable or even increase in the long term. Studies have shown that married couples tend to have higher levels of happiness than singles or people in other marital statuses (Clark & Georgellis, 2013; Grover & Helliwell, 2019; Lucas et al., 2003; Zimmermann & Easterlin, 2006). The use of panel data and refined empirical methods has also made it possible to disambiguate the causal relationship in the relationship between marriage and happiness, showing that it is actually marriage that makes spouses happier, not that happy people marry more often (Grover & Helliwell, 2019; Stutzer & Frey, 2006).

In a recent paper, Murro et al. (2023), using ISTAT data that measure subjective well-being in its various dimensions (satisfaction with the economic situation, health, relationship with family and friends, work and leisure), show that married and cohabiting couples are more likely to be satisfied with their health and their relationships with family and friends. On the other hand, singles are more likely to be satisfied with their free time and work. This study shows that the intensity of bonding, as measured by marital status, the presence of children and religiosity, is positively correlated with almost all dimensions of well-being. There is a positive effect of children on the well-being of families, which is ambivalent and depends on both the type of family and the area of satisfaction considered. In other words, the effect of children can vary depending on the specific dynamics of the family and the different dimensions of well-being that are considered.

This empirical evidence also has important implications for family policy in the broader context of public policy. In fact, there has long been empirical evidence in developed countries showing that the relationship between economic growth and happiness reaches a saturation point at which the increase in income does not necessarily lead to a proportional increase in happiness (Easterlin, 1974). Hence the idea that public policy should consider happiness as a primary goal that goes beyond mere economic growth. And if strong family ties are one of the most important determinants of happiness, then family policy becomes one of the surprisingly direct instruments of economic policy. In summary: More families, more happiness, more health!

Families, Children, Birth Rates and the Sustainability of the Welfare State

The issue of children and the birth rate is of central importance, especially in a country like Italy, which has long since entered a deep demographic winter. In this section, we want to address at least one economic aspect, why families have hardly had children for several years, and what needs to change in families to increase the birth rate.

If we were to ask what a family produces, the short answer would be: children. According to Becker and Barro (1986), the net benefit of the family results from the contribution of the parents and the children. The idea that parents engender children

for selfish reasons in order to benefit from them makes children a private good in the economic sense of the word. Nancy Folbre (1994), on the other hand, emphasized the altruistic and social component of children. Children are a public good, as they represent the future of a country's workforce. Adequate education and training for young people helps to create a skilled and productive population that can support economic growth and innovation. Children also ensure the sustainability of the welfare system in countries where the pay-as-you-go system is based on the principle of intergenerational solidarity and where younger generations work and pay taxes to support the well-being of older generations. After all, children contribute to innovation and economic growth through new ideas, talents and skills. The new generations bring new perspectives and skills that can drive technological development and innovation in various sectors. By characterizing children as a public good, Folbre (1994) wanted to emphasize that their existence - which is due to the economic effort of parents - has positive effects on society as a whole and therefore also on those who did not want or could not have children. From this disproportion between the private costs of parents and the public benefits for all, arises the problem of underproduction and the need for public intervention that collectivizes the costs of "production" through taxes. This new perspective also helps in part to understand one of the roots of low fertility and possibly find a solution. Horizontal fiscal justice measures such as tax deductions or child benefits are therefore the direct response of economic policy to the problem of "underproduction" of children.

But there is more. Until a few decades ago, the link between marriage and fertility was taken for granted, to the point where demographers used the age of marriage as one of the determining variables for predicting the fertility rate. Over time, the explosion in the number of extramarital pregnancies – in some European countries more than half of all births – has cast doubt on this link. It will therefore be interesting to examine what the fertility rate is as a function of marital status. Although the analysis is technically complicated, empirical evidence shows that there is still a positive association between stable family bonding and fertility (Hoem et al., 2013; O'Leary et al., 2010; Stone & Spencer, 2022). In this case, too, the implications for a government family policy are relevant, as they indicate that public policies to strengthen and improve family ties also indirectly favour the birth rate. More family, more future generations.

More information about the author via the QR code:
www.familyvalued.org/Matteo-Rizzolli-2

Dr. Wido Geis-Thöne

Senior Economist for Family Policy
and Migration Issues
Institut der deutschen Wirtschaft
Germany

Families are decisive for Germany's long-term economic success / Family as a location factor

Abstract

As tomorrow's skilled workers, children shape the long-term development of growth and prosperity in Germany. Not only their number but also their successful education is of decisive importance. A good development environment for children is therefore advantageous to the economy also. However, family policy benefits that start today only pay off after decades. Therefore, family policy often has a very difficult passage through the legislature, especially in unfavourable budgetary situations.

Article

In recent years, shortages of skilled workers have become an ever-greater obstacle to the performance of the German economy, and the situation is likely to worsen significantly with the retirement of the baby boomers of the 1950s and 1960s. At the same time, public budgets are likely to become increasingly imbalanced, as more and more people in the pay-as-you-go social security system receive a statutory pension, and fewer employees remain to finance it with their contributions. The reason for these developments is that the number of births between 1964 and 1975 collapsed from 1.36 million to only 780,000 and since then has never even come close to the level of population sustenance. For a long time, this had hardly any negative

economic consequences, as the proportion of the labour force in the population re-mained high. In the meantime, however, a tipping point has been passed, and the demographic structure is shifting more and more towards older people who are no longer active in the labour market.

On the one hand, this shows how important families are for long-term economic success. On the other hand, however, it is also becoming clear how long the conse-quences of unfavourable developments take to become noticeable. For example, most of the politicians who could have shaped a different family policy environment in the 1960s and 1970s are not even alive today. Even if the positive economic effects of strengthening families become noticeable when children enter the labour market, that does not happen until one-and-a-half to two decades after their birth, at the earliest. Such measures do not usually pay off within the short political planning horizons of one-to-two legislative periods. Family policies are unpopular because their costs are generally immediate, whereas their positive effects lie largely in a distant, barely foreseeable future. The responsible political players are not even always aware that the support of families is an investment. However, especially in times of tight budgets, it is necessary to keep it in mind in order to avoid false economies.

In order to secure growth and prosperity in Germany, it is not enough to enable the people in the country to have as many children as they wish. It is also important that the children find the best possible developmental environment. There is a lot to be done here, as the negative trends in student performance tests, such as PISA, make clear. At the same time, the economy is already primarily lacking well-trained specialists, and the importance of qualifications is likely to increase even further with the advance of digitization and automation. In this context, people who develop in-novative products and services, and found innovative companies, are particularly im-portant for the economic success of a country. Family policy has a particularly strong influence on the development of children's skills in the pre-school sector through childcare facilities. If they do not acquire sufficient German language skills to be able to follow school lessons well from the start, it can have a very negative impact on their educational careers in the long term. At the same time, however, support for families to handle German half-day schooling is also of great importance for the learning success of older children.

In this context, the compatibility of family and career, which has been considered in more detail elsewhere, must be kept in mind. Given the existing shortage of skilled workers, it is very important for Germany's economic development that mothers and fathers are able to pursue gainful employment to the greatest possible extent.

More information about the author via the QR code:
www.familyvalued.org/Wido-Geis-Thoene-2

Hartmut Steeb

Secretary-General of the
Evangelical Alliance in Deutschland
(retired)
Germany

Family – the original solution to loneliness

Abstract

The German government has, for the first time, launched a "Loneliness Monitor". Unsurprisingly it finds, among other things, that single parents suffer significantly more loneliness than non-single parents. Is that any wonder? For decades there has been a media barrage against marriage and the traditional family. Then the tables were turned, and today they raise to the status of marriage unions other than the established heterosexual marriage based on fidelity and reliability. And then they redefine the concept of family as wherever children and adults live together.

Article

Apparently, the increase in loneliness is a new major problem for postmodern society. Even state institutions already see it as a new task for society as a whole, not to simply leave loneliness alone, but to develop counterstrategies, set up projects, and hire consultants.

I propose that we focus once more on the natural, original and sustainable concept of humanity: marriage – the lifelong partnership of love and fidelity between a man and a woman, who spend not just a particular period of their lives together but promise and commit themselves to each other for their entire lives. "Until death do you part" was, and is, God's promised blessing for that commitment. And ideally,

children will arise through the sexual union that is also cultivated by this marital union. This is how a marriage becomes a family.

Family comes from the Latin root Famulus and means 'community of service'. Humans are not naturally solitary creatures. The book of Genesis already affirms that "it is not good for man to be alone". That is why humanity exists in two types, as man and as woman. But even these two should not live only for themselves but have the task of co-creation: "Be fruitful and multiply; fill the earth and subdue it". The sexes' natural gifts and talents oblige them to shape the future in authentic sustainability: in other words, to ensure that human life continues after them. If today, for the sake of the future, certain people think they need to call for a "birth strike", then they have not understood that shaping the future needs nothing more urgently than people!

"Marriage and family are THE alternatives to egotism and egocentricity, to excessive self-determination and self-realization, to a fatherless, motherless and futureless society"

Family is THE alternative to egotism and egocentricity, to excessive self-determination and self-realization. Those who care only about themselves, their advancement and self-development in mind will ultimately reap what they have sown: themselves alone, that is, loneliness! The family is that small social unit in which life is formed. Here you learn to be considerate. Here you can relax after stress. Here you can gather new strength for the everyday challenges of coping with life. Here you complement each other's talents. Here you share joy and sorrow with each other. Together we master the task of life from birth to death. Yes, it is also a task that often requires hard work, but we humans are not in the world to do nothing. Children are a challenge, and they also challenge their parents because we often rediscover our own faults in them. As our 13-year-old once said: "Don't put so much effort into raising us, we're only going to become like you anyway!" Indeed, you can hear it said that upbringing is futile because the children imitate their parents anyway. So children can mature through their parents, but also parents through their children. In the family the goal is not to 'get your money's worth', but to help fellow family members to live and develop to their full potential.

Two other people made it possible for me to live. Is it not then the very minimum that gratitude demands that we in turn make it possible for at least two other people to live? Nowadays people are mainly concerned with how to avoid the responsibility of children as far as possible. We are wrong to talk about 'family planning' when we actually mean only 'family prevention'. One's main responsibility is precisely to provide for one's own offspring. This is how to live naturally and sustainably.

A few years ago, the Allensbach opinion research institute asked the question who the happiest people are, and the astonishing result was: young parents with small children.

I asked myself, "Wait a minute, what was it like when the children were small? Wasn't it a 365-day on-call service, day and night?" It was a time without any real holiday, especially for the mother – who is constantly in demand. Since my wife and I have 10 children, I can say that we probably never got an uninterrupted night's sleep for almost 20 years. And that's supposed to be the happiest time?

Surprisingly – yes!

Surprisingly, the most arduous task in the family, caring for children, never prevents us from being happy. And they can now pass on something of the life they received. This gives us all meaningfulness, happiness and satisfaction.

Alexander Mitscherlich warned against the fatherless society. That was a long time ago. This fatherless society has been followed to a large extent by a motherless society, which then naturally leads to a childless society, and ultimately to a society without a future. It is high time for a course correction.

More information about the author via the QR code:
www.familyvalued.org/Hartmut-Steeb-2

4 Family-Career Balance

Birgit Wintermann
Bertelsmann Stiftung
Senior Project Manager
Sustainable Economic program
Germany

Dorothee Kubitza
Bertelsmann Stiftung
Project Assistant
Sustainable Economic program
Germany

The Future of Work: A World Where Family Matters

Abstract

In the period from 2011 to 2022, the Bertelsmann Foundation offered certification of companies as "Family-Friendly Employers". In the process, the culture of the companies was examined in particular. It was shown that family-friendly companies not only achieve a better family-work balance for their employees, but they are also more future-proof.

Article

Wednesday morning, 10 a.m. "A quick cup of coffee before we start," Max thinks. Carefully he leans his crutches against the kitchen counter and supports himself so as not to strain his freshly operated leg. He stretches with difficulty and takes the coffee container out of the cupboard – almost empty. Suddenly a crash ... the crutches fall to the floor. "What a bummer." Helplessly, Max clings to the counter. At this moment, the key turns in the door – his best friend Sebastian greets him with a cheerful hello. And with the purchases ... as well as two fragrant mugs of coffee. They drink them together before Sebastian accompanies him to his appointment at the hospital and then has to go back to work.

Family-friendliness: work and family in harmony

What does this story have to do with family-friendliness? One friend supports another who depends on it, thanks perhaps to flexible working hours. Does that make Sebastian's work results worse? Probably not! Is he more motivated to work for a tolerant employer? Probably yes!

Those who succeed in reconciling work and family life for their employees can benefit. In order to master challenges in a sustainable way, motivated specialists are necessary - who are often rare. The solution can be to reintegrate qualified employees with family responsibilities into the companies. If they focus on family-friendliness, they show that they go beyond traditional working models and create a culture of trust, flexibility and appreciation. Family-friendliness thus becomes a competitive advantage. Companies not only strengthen their image but also promote positive social development.

But Max and Sebastian are just friends – what's 'family' about that? Over time family structures have changed completely, and it is not just about people with whom you are connected in the narrower sense. Today's understanding is more like this: family is everyone for whom you feel responsible. There might even be "parental leave" to house-train a puppy!

A certificate for family-friendliness

The Bertelsmann Stiftung has taken up the issue and awarded a certificate for companies, the Family-Friendly Employer Quality Seal, from 2011 to 2022. Developed from a partnership with the project "Family, Work and Medium-Sized Businesses in Münsterland", it successfully certified 420 companies from various industries throughout Germany, 35 percent of them were even seeking renewal.

The aim was to qualitatively evaluate the fami y-friendliness of the companies. For this purpose, both employers and all employees were surveyed by means of a questionnaire - supplemented by one or two workshops, and interviews with individual employees. Five differently weighted criteria were used for the evaluation: communication, corporate and management culture, work organization, support services, as well as strategy and sustainability. The results were considered against the background of the following questions and thus an individual benchmark was created:

1)   What industry is it and how is work primarily done there? In manufacturing activities, e.g. on machines? In office jobs that permit mobile working? In sales activities that require customer contact?

2)   Where is the company located (rural, urban, in conurbations)?

3)   How much does the company try to accommodate its employees in terms of family-work balance?

The overall assessment finally led to the assessment of whether the company can be considered family-friendly and so receive the certificate (Seal of Quality - Family-Friendly Employers of the Bertelsmann Foundation).

What did we learn from this?

Mindset over Measures

The decisive factor for the evaluation was not only the measures and their effort, but rather how much effort was made to meet the needs of the employees - taking into account the respective circumstances: Even if remote work is not possible in a butcher's shop, the company can act in an employee-oriented way - e.g. by making work schedules flexible and paying tax-free care allowances. This requires a value-oriented

mindset that considers employees as individuals, not as interchangeable "human resources". Good, open communication as well as a trusting and approachable culture are of greater importance than glossy brochures about parent-child rooms.

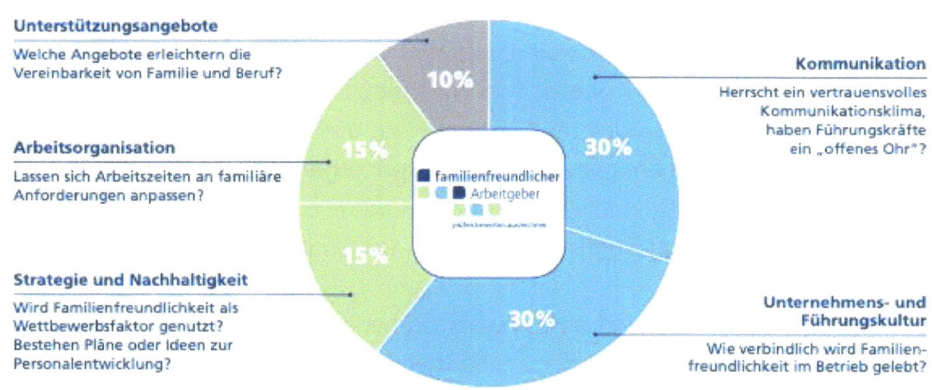

Source: Bertelsmann Foundation

Adaptation for the future

Family-friendly companies are experts in troubleshooting and prove themselves particularly adaptable by matching the needs of employees with company requirements. They are also better able to master the digital and sustainability transformations, key issues for the coming years. The focus is on people - those who live this ethic are also concerned about such topics as (social) sustainability. In fact, everything is done to realize both together.

In times where challenges are increasing, it is the employee-oriented companies that motivate and empower their workforce to drive innovation together - a strategy that ensures the company's long-term success.

Family-friendliness and employee orientation - not an end in itself

The success of a company depends to a large extent on the ability of people with individual needs and areas of life to pursue a common goal without disadvantaging others. Success should be measured not only by financial indicators, but also by the common good. This mindset is critical to confidently meeting the challenges of the future, and actively contributing to shaping a better world that goes beyond the business environment.

More information about the authors via the QR code:
www.familyvalued.org/Birgit-Wintermann-2

http://www.familyvalued.org/Dorothee-Kubitza-2

Dagmar Weßler-Poßberg
Head of Politic Business
Prognos AG
Germany

Employees – not recipients but active shapers of family-work balance

Abstract

"Do good and talk about it", this recipe for high employer attractiveness is already well known with respect to the compatibility of family and career. Many companies have established a wide variety of media and formats for communicating their offers for family-work balance. Not least because of the Corona pandemic, employees have learned to actively approach the company with their compatibility of family and career needs, to demand support and to propose their own solutions. Family-work compatibility as a shared responsibility, i.e. recognizing employees as competent agents who not only cross the boundaries between work and family on a daily basis but also want to shape and manage them according to their own ideas. If family-work balance solutions are to be positive for employees and companies, it is worthwhile to listen to what mothers, fathers and caregivers want, and to promote family-work management that is profitable for families and companies through suitable family-work balance offers. So, what do mothers and fathers want? Here are a few statistics.

Article

Meaningfulness, freedom, personal responsibility and development – these principles of "New Work" should be realizable through flexible working hours and

telecommuting, among other things. But wait a minute! Didn't we want to talk about reconciling work and family? What does New Work have to do with it?

"But not only the meaningfulness of work is subject to change, but also the ideas about the relationship between work and private life and thus also the expectations of compatibility."

A lot, because both in New Work and in family-work compatibility, employees with their expectations and needs are the focus of attention. While New Work is understood as a change process in which a fresh wind is blowing, the concept of family-work compatibility is perhaps a bit dusty. New Work aims to change the expectations and needs of employees. New Work concepts are intended to open room for manoeuvre and creative freedom for meaningful work from which employees and companies benefit. Some companies at least have realized that this cultural change is not possible on behalf of employees, but only together with them; and a participatory decision-making process makes it possible.

Employees and companies alike benefit from a successful family-work balance. However, family-work compatibility is rarely considered from the point of view of change. What mothers need for a good family-work balance is well-known and can also be implemented for fathers. At least that's how it appears when you look at the usual range of measures. However, it is not only the meaningfulness of work that is subject to change but also the ideas about the relationship between work and private life and thus the expectations of family-work compatibility. The coronavirus pandemic has given this long-term development a strong boost, and it has taught us that working parents are not simply passive recipients of family-work balance offers, but active agents who want to shape and manage the boundaries between work and family according to their own ideas.

There are spatial boundaries between the home and the office or factory floor, working hours form time limits, values and rules in the family and at work set the dividing lines for appropriate behaviour. Parents and employees with care responsibilities organize these boundaries between work and family every day throughout life, using the opportunities available to them.

"All employees expect fundamental consideration for their compatibility requirements."

And here it is already clear that family-work balances can differ. In the lives of women and men, different needs and priorities arise in the course of their lives. Perhaps the mother who has been working part-time for many years wants to start again full-time when the child is older, or the highly committed manager temporarily needs a flexible part-time model to ensure the care of disabled parents.

Both for New Work and family-work compatibility, flexibility is considered the panacea for the working world of tomorrow. However, the forms of this flexibility are as diverse and individual as the employees themselves. Flexible and fluid working hours and locations, or rather a plannable end to the working day and sacrosanct family time – requirements and their corresponding measures vary over the course of life, depending on the life situation and the relative importance of work and private life that derives from it. According to a representative survey, 42 percent of employees with family responsibilities feel that flexible working times are best for their own family-work balance, whereas 21 percent prefer the highest possible predictability afforded by fixed working hours (1).

In principle, all employees expect their family-work requirements to be considered. In terms of flexibility however, mothers, fathers and family caregivers (still) have different priorities. Mothers, who are still mainly responsible for childcare, find it particularly important to reduce working hours and to work hours that they can adapt to the opening hours of daycare centres and schools. Fathers, on the other hand, are more inclined towards flexible working time models such as flexitime, with which they can reduce working hours on particular days of the week. Caregivers, on the one hand, need flexibility to be able to react whenever necessary and in emergencies. On the other hand, their working hours are precisely aligned their care responsibilities, so that overtime or spontaneous changes in working hours can be problematic (2).

Experience from the world of work during the Corona pandemic shows us how family-work compatibility can be individually customized without becoming an excessive burden for companies:

"Employees as active shapers of their family-work compatibility"

61

Employees have learned to address their family-work balance needs pro-actively: The pandemic has challenged parents to take action themselves in addressing their family-work requirements. In representative studies with around 2500 parents (3), almost half of the parents with children under the age of 15 stated that they had approached their employer themselves to find and to agree on solutions for the loss of childcare. And they had predominantly positive experiences in doing that. This is because 81 percent of parents who negotiated with their employer received support. Half experienced their employer as accommodating, and 31 percent, though not exactly met with enthusiasm from the employer, still received support (4).

Through open exchange, managers and employees become a strategic team in finding individual options: Companies that established active communication about family-work compatibility needs experienced working parents as constructive partners even in the crisis. In two out of three companies (62%) with active communication on the topic of family-work balance, parents actively worked out solutions. Among companies without active communication, the figure was only half as high (33%) (5).

It is therefore worthwhile to get employees on board as active shapers of their own family-work balances. After all, balance is not a "nice to have" that companies grant, but a crucial consideration for busy parents. The employment of around 11.6 million working parents with children under the age of 16 in Germany is influenced by this. Among them are 7.3 million parents with more than one child, 3.2 million where the youngest child is under 3 years of age, and almost one million single parents. In addition, there are almost 2.5 million employed people who care for relatives.

Literature

(1) Prognos: Familienfreundliche Arbeitgeber. Die Attraktivitätsstudie 2024)
(2) dto.
(3) Prognos 2021: Erfahrungen und neue Impulse für die betriebliche Vereinbarkeitspolitik, für das BMFSFJ
(4) Allensbacher Archiv, IfD-Umfragen 8262 (2021). Darstellung Prognos AG. Prognos-Studie aus der Corona-Krise lernen

(5) Prognos 2021: Erfahrungen und neue Impulse für die betriebliche Vereinbarkeitspolitik, für das BMFSFJ

More information about the author via the QR code:

www.familyvalued.org/Dagmar-Wessler-Possberg-2

**Elke Sieber und
Daniel Wensauer-Sieber**

Managing Partners

swsp-transform

Germany

Entrepreneurial couple – An underestimated life and work model

Abstract

When we set out as a couple to start a company in 2016, our son was six years old. With this form of joint business management on equal terms, we combined the compatibility of a happy marriage with self-realization as parents and with a meaningful professional life. We have continued to develop this iconic triangle and thus try to bring a healthy balance between the couple's relationship, family and professional life. This has worked out for us.

In this article we present our vision for the foundation of our family and our company; how we pursue together the path of continuous development on a professional and private level; and what dreams and goals we still have.

We would also like to encourage other couples to start a business together.

Article

In 2016, we - a couple with a six-year-old son at the time - set out to start a company: leave regular employment, develop a business idea, write a business plan and get into entrepreneurship - without a safety net. Our goal was to combine happy coupledom, self-realization as parents and family, and a rewarding professional life. This triangle of couple's relationship, family and professional life is still the basis of our life

and work today. We are constantly developing and trimming the balance of the three components of this triangle.

The vision of our family and business foundation

Our vision was to create a company that is not only economically successful but also makes a positive contribution to society. We wanted to create a working environment where we could express ourselves as a couple and a family without any of us having to take a back seat. For this reason, we have taken the time to develop a vision. And since pictures say more than words, the basis was postcards, from which we selected pictures or image sections that fit our ideas, wishes and goals. After many discussions, refinements and changes, we asked a "graphic recorder" to translate this into a picture for us – this is how our mission statement was created, in which everything starts from the aforementioned triangle of couple's relationship, family and professional life.

Explanation of the graphic: From postcard to designed vision: A vision as a starting point for our path as an entrepreneurial couple.

By the way, our attempt to find information or literature about entrepreneurial couples was not very successful – there were a few articles, very little literature and generally unhelpful information.

The path of continuous development

The founding and management of a company is a continuous process of further development. We have learned that it is important to pause again and again, to reflect and to make adjustments where necessary. In doing so, we have always tried to reconcile our private and professional goals. So we are continuously balancing the triangle described above, because needs change and necessities change through the development of our son. The words daycare, school, secondary school, indicate only one sphere of these changing needs.

In the graphic this 'Reflexion' is symbolized by the tree, the table and the bottle of wine. The way forward is clearly recognizable and shows the future, which in French stands for the planned future. Our attitude to the future can be described quite well with the quote of the well-known management thinker Peter F. Drucker: "The best way to predict the future is to shape it". Our French neighbours have another word for the future: Avenir. A future that is coming our way: unplanned, unwanted and sometimes challenging. We all remember Corona, for example. It was a challenge that initially presented us with many problems because many orders were lost in our consulting business. Online was the new normal and school closures were a new situation. One month after lockdown, after numerous joint discussions and some YouTube videos about online tools, we adapted to the new situation and gradually brought our triangle back into balance.

Our Dreams and Goals

Even after several years of running the company, we still have many dreams and goals. We want to continue to expand our company and realize new projects, while always maintaining our values and principles, and keeping family and partnership in mind.

We would also like to encourage other couples to run a business together and as equal partners – or at least to consider that as a possible option. It is a challenge, but also a great opportunity to combine work and family, to create something together, and to experience a continuous learning curve together. Entrepreneurial couples face unique challenges, but with the right attitude, clear communication and mutual support, entrepreneurial couples gain a lot of freedom as well as creative possibilities. We have been experiencing for years that we can bundle our strengths in this way and work together towards our goals. With this in mind: take the plunge and start a company together! It is worth it as a couple, as a family and for a fulfilling professional life.

Starting a business as a couple? These are the important Dos and Don'ts
Dos

1) Communication: Communication is key to any healthy relationship, both business and personal. Talk regularly about your goals, plans and concerns to avoid

misunderstandings; and make decisions together – we have developed a morning ritual for this.

2) Role distribution: Define clear roles and responsibilities within the company, to avoid conflicts and collaborate efficiently. Each partner should know which tasks they are taking on, and how these complement each other.

3) Respect: Respect your partner's opinions, ideas, and ways of working. Show appreciation for their work and support each other in difficult situations – and experience shows that these difficult situations always arise.

4) Leisure and work: Be sure to find a healthy balance between work and personal life. Make time for joint activities outside the company to strengthen the relationship and reduce stress.

5) Shared goals: Define common goals and visions for your organization, to stay motivated and collaborate successfully. Work on a long-term strategy based on the interests of both partners. Our vision carries us along and continues to this day as the basis for development.

6) Flexibility: Be flexible and open to changes in your business and your relationship. Adapt to new challenges and develop solutions to problems together.

7) Self-care: Don't forget to take care of yourself and take time for your own personal development. Make sure that both your physical and your mental health are in balance.

Don'ts

1) Don't ignore conflicts: Avoid ignoring or sweeping under the rug conflicts or problems in your partnership. Communicate openly and constructively about your concerns in order to clarify misunderstandings at an early stage.

2) Don't neglect the separation between work and private life: Try to separate work and private life to find a healthy balance. Avoid constantly talking about business matters and consciously take time for joint activities outside the company.

3) Don't make one-sided decisions: Don't make important decisions unilaterally without involving your partner. Respect your partner's opinions and ideas and work together on solutions.

4) Don't blame: Avoid blaming your partner for problems in the company. Instead, look for constructive solutions and work together to overcome challenges.

5) Don't neglect clear communication: Communicate clearly with each other to avoid misunderstandings. Make sure that both partners know what is expected of them and what goals they are pursuing together.

6) Don't neglect your relationship: Take time for your partnership and invest in maintaining your relationship. Show interest in your partner's life and support each other in all areas of life.

7) Don't exert excessive pressure: Don't pressure each other or expect unrealistic performance from each other. Accept each other's limitations and support each other in difficult times. Being an entrepreneurial couple means embarking on a long journey together, starting with the first step.

More information about the authors via the QR code:
www.familyvalued.org/Elke-Sieber-2

www.familyvalued.org/Daniel-Wensauer-Sieber-2

Katja Kaltenbach
Founder
kiwifalter
Germany

Stephanie Maus
Founder
kiwifalter
Germany

kiwifalter – the hub for pioneering family-work balance

Abstract

Healthy societies of tomorrow need happy families today. Families are looking for real places that support them in all phases of life: pregnancy, parental leave, daycare and primary school; and finally, Article.

Family Hub – Childcare 2.0

Young parents want both careers and children, which makes everyday life a challenge. The return to work after parental leave is particularly stressful, as there are neither sufficient nor flexible childcare places for children under the age of three. Daycare centres, large daycare centres and childminders cover basic care but do not meet the requirements of the modern world of work.

71

The high demand for daycare places often leads to long waiting lists. Even with a place, parents often experience inflexibility and a lack of reliability. When working from home, parents with small children want to be close to them, which daycare centres cannot provide. Childminders are a more flexible alternative, but often not available on a stable basis.

The Family Hub kiwifalter offers an innovative solution: it combines childcare and workplaces under one roof, which can be booked individually and flexibly via an app. Parents can work in kiwifalter's coworking space, while their children are looked after in the in-house Kids Space. Being close to the child enables a gentle return to work and ensures a high level of employee satisfaction and loyalty when the children move on to secondary schools. What used to be done by large families or village communities is now done by the family hub kiwifalter. Flexible payment and booking models via an app complete this innovative concept of diverse family-work compatibility tools under one roof, a concept which is used by families and companies alike.

Family Hub - Coworking und Learning Space

More and more start-ups, self-employed people and employees appreciate the flexibility and creative atmosphere of coworking spaces. As places of lived New Work culture, they offer a cost-effective alternative to conventional offices and promote networking and exchange.

The Family Hub goes one step further and combines coworking with flexible childcare. Parents benefit from a professional workspace including Kids Space and a lively community. Since the opening of kiwifalter in 2019, this dynamic community has seen numerous start-ups.

kiwifalter responds to the needs of modern families and, in addition to reconciling work and family, also offers courses and workshops in art, music, fitness, languages and mindfulness for children and adults.

The kiwifalter company

Currently, families with children are the main clientele of kiwifalter. However, companies, especially small and medium-sized enterprises (SMEs), also recognize the advantages of kiwifalter. A company-internal daycare centre is often not affordable for SMEs. The kiwifalter alternative offers flexible and cost-effective childcare in coworking format. The childcare times can be arranged individually at kiwifalter and booked flexibly via Kids Space cards or on a subscription basis.

A use case: A company promoted an employee with two small children to a management position. The mother was already using kiwifalter's Family coworking for her first child. When she was pregnant with her 2nd child her company booked a childcare package for her directly with kiwifalter. In this way, the company ensured that the employee was best able to reconcile work and family life and do justice to the management position – this is exactly the core idea of kiwifalter.

One Hub for all: holistic family life offer

With the age of the children, the needs of the families also change. kiwifalter supports them with appropriate offers depending on their phase of life, ranging from flexible childcare to educational offers and holiday camps to homework supervision. The one-stop-shop concept reduces the number of interfaces to one and offers clear added value for families and companies.

In contrast to daycare centres, only the times actually spent in family coworking are charged. In addition, the flexibility to take advantage of the offer soon after birth offers parents a completely new perspective on the compatibility of family and career, long before traditional daycare centres come into question.

kiwifalter's vision extends beyond its current location in Düsseldorf. In future, the childcare offered within the framework of coworking, which is mainly used by parents with very young children, is to be expanded to include a daycare centre in kiwifalter and expanded nationwide through strategic partnerships.

More information about the authors via the QR code:
www.familyvalued.org/Katja-Kaltenbach-2

www.familyvalued.org/Stephanie-Maus-2

Angelika Beierlein
COO
Evernine Group
Germany

Hannes Beierlein
CEO
Evernine Group
Germany

Partnership, kids, career – Our Path as an equal entrepreneurial couple

Abstract

In this article, Geli (Angelika) and Hannes describe how they master the balance between traditional family values and modern equality. As equal partners in their professional and private lives, they run their own company and share responsibilities at home. The chapter shows how they overcome conflicts and create added value for their families through compromises and joint decisions. A straightforward narrative about the interplay of give and take in a partnership that questions and redefines traditional role models.

Article
Rethinking success and family

We, Hannes and Angelika Beierlein, are not only an entrepreneurial couple but also parents of two small children – Fabian (4 years) and Toni (1 year). Our everyday life is characterized by the challenge of reconciling work and family. With our 50/50 model, we have a progressive and innovative solution that meets both our professional and family obligations, without disadvantaging either of us. Our story should not only encourage other entrepreneurial couples, but also couples in top management, to follow this groundbreaking path.

Our vision and motivation

From the very beginning we had a clear vision: to form a company that is economically successful and at the same time enables us to have an equal partnership and to offer our children a loving environment. "We wanted to create an environment in which we could both be successful professionally and can take care of our children equally," explains Hannes. This vision goes far beyond traditional roles. In addition to our jobs we also share common hobbies such as skydiving and kitesurfing. These exciting activities help us to stay connected as a couple and to live intense experiences together. We believe that neither professional nor private obligations should suffer as a result. These shared adventures strengthen our relationship and give us energy for everyday life.

Continuous development and adaptation

Founding and running a business requires constant adaptation and development. "It is important to regularly pause and reflect on whether our way of working still corresponds to our private and professional goals," emphasizes Angelica. We attach great importance to re-setting our own goals and satisfaction criteria again and again. Through continuous adjustments we have managed to reconcile our professional and family obligations. A clear distribution of roles and regular communication are indispensable for this.

We have established fixed times in which we devote ourselves exclusively to the family or to work. One daily ritual is our breakfast together, where we discuss our challenges and plans for the day. This routine strengthens our partnership and helps us to spend the day in a structured and coordinated way. In addition, we hold a weekly "Jour Fixe" on Sunday evenings, where we plan the week and discuss any deviations from the routine.

Scientific evidence

Scientific studies show that an equal distribution of the tasks in the family not only increases the satisfaction of the partners but also has a positive impact on children's development. Children living in an environment in which both parents work equally and take care of them, often show greater emotional stability and better social skills (Pew Research Centre).

Challenges and solutions

Of course, there are also challenges. "One of the biggest challenges is the separation of work and private life," explains Hannes. We have fixed times in which there is only family time and times in which we can concentrate on work. However, we do not strictly separate work and private life as we both enjoy our work, and it is an integral part of our lives – something that is especially important for entrepreneurs and executives. This model has helped us to be productive and still spend enough time with our children.

Another obstacle is flexibility in everyday work. "Sometimes we have to react quickly to unexpected events, whether in the company or with the children," says Angelika. Flexibility and mutual support are therefore essential.

Our 50/50 model means that we actually measure the time required for individual tasks, so we can spot an imbalance. We share equally the picking-up of the children from kindergarten, the housework and the planning of activities with family and friends. Deviations from this routine we discuss as part of our weekly "Jour Fixe" on Sunday evenings.

Positive examples and inspiration

Despite the challenges, we see many advantages in our way of life. "We want to encourage other couples to try it too. It's not always easy, but the reward is worth

it," says Hannes. Our story shows that it is possible to run a company successfully as an equal couple, while at the same time having a happy family.

Our 10 tips for a successful family-work balance

1) Communication: Regular and open discussions about goals, plans and concerns are essential. We have developed a morning ritual for this, where we plan our day and discuss possible challenges.

2) Clear distribution of roles: Each of us has clear responsibilities, both in the company as well as at home. This avoids conflicts and ensures efficient collaboration.

3) Respect and appreciation: We respect the opinions, ideas and working methods of the other. Appreciation and support in difficult situations are crucial.

4) Fixed times for family and work: We have defined clear times in which we dedicate ourselves exclusively to family or work. Thus, we ensure that we work productively as well as spending quality time with our children. 5. Flexibility: Flexibility and the ability to adapt to new situations are essential. We react quickly to unexpected events, be they at the company or with the children.

6) Shared vision and goals: We have a long-term strategy based on the interests of both partners. This shared vision motivates us and gives us orientation.

7) Taking care of ourselves: We take time for our own personal development and take care of our physical and mental health. This is how we stay balanced and able to support each other better.

8) Work and private life in harmony: Even though we have fixed times for family and work, we integrate our work into our private lives, because we enjoy work and because it is part of our identity. We like to talk about our projects and ideas, and this further strengthens our partnership.

9) Constructive conflict resolution: We speak openly and constructively about conflicts and problems. In this way we avoid misunderstandings and find solutions together.

10) Investing in the marriage partnership: We take time for our marriage partnership and actively cultivate it. Joint activities outside the company strengthen our relationship and help us reduce stress.

Summary

Our journey as an entrepreneurial couple shows that it is possible to reconcile work and family on an equitable basis. The right attitude, clear communication and mutual support help us attain both professional success and family satisfaction. We hope that our story inspires other couples to follow similar paths and enjoy the advantages of an equal partnership.

Sources:

1. Couples' Division of Employment and Household Chores and Relationship Satisfaction
2. How Men and Women View Family Life, Household Duties During COVID-19
3. How an Unfair Division of Labor Hurts Your Relationship
4. Men Say They Are Spending More Time on Household Chores

More information about the authors via the QR code:
www.familyvalued.org/Angelika-Beierlein-2

www.familyvalued.org/Hannes-Beierlein-2

Kiki Radicke
Head of People & Culture
Adacor Hosting GmbH
Germany

Reconciling family and career — a win-win-win situation

Abstract

When it is possible to reconcile family and career, everyone benefits — companies, employees and children. With only little effort, but the right mindset and the right measures, companies can not only increase employee satisfaction, reduce staff turnover and increase productivity, but also create a working environment with security and social care, in which career and family go hand in hand. Read about the measures we have implemented at Adacor, a medium-sized IT service provider, and what results we have achieved.

Article

The balance between professional and private life is no longer considered a mere "nice to have". It has become a decisive economic factor. This opens up numerous opportunities for companies: Those who successfully implement a family-work balance become a magnet for talent and build an image as a sought-after, family-friendly employer.

Let's look at working time models in a new light: Flexible design allows skilled workers to shine not only in their careers, but also in their private lives. Why shouldn't every position also be offered part-time? The need for management positions is growing, as is the implementation of tandem models. The extended target group ensures

that highly qualified candidates are quickly hired; it enriches team diversity and fuels the company's innovative strength.

At Adacor, it has been shown that a parent-child office directly at the company's location provides relief in childcare emergencies – a pragmatic interim solution that has parents' backs without sacrificing vacation days. It is striking that fathers in particular appreciate this offer, as it enables them to spend quality time with their children and to live a more balanced care work.

Parent and care mentors are not only a support in challenging times, they also act as ambassadors for the family-work compatibility concept. Through their work, an awareness is created in the team; they design tailor-made offers and remain reliable points of contact for topics relating to family and care. Adacor has prepared fertile terrain for these mentors: Our leadership guidelines bear their mark.

Everyday work can be demanding. However, agile methods such as sprint planning, well-timed core times for meetings and an online-first strategy create an organizational structure that avoids overload and leaves time for private life. An open coaching offer that also accommodates personal concerns has a preventive effect against stress and burn-out – employees remain resilient, downtimes are reduced, and general satisfaction grows.

Pregnancy and parental leave feel like goodbyes at many companies. At Adacor, we have turned this around: Parental leave does not mean isolation, but becomes part of personal development, supplemented by further training opportunities and coaching. By planning the career path during pregnancy, we retain skilled workers and, above all, allow women in particular a seamless return to work. A well-thought-out parental leave process accompanies employees before, during and after this phase, so that the connection to the team is never broken. This not only bonds parents with the company and shortens absences; it also saves recruiting costs and training times for new employees.

Our Steps Career Framework offers a wide range of career opportunities based on five qualities: technical skill, team success, strategic thinking, responsibility, and development. The performance of the employees, their positive influence and their effectiveness in the company are evaluated and classified, regardless of their weekly working hours. This enables individual careers that fit the respective life situation and a fair evaluation of performance: a tool that helps to prevent gender pay-gaps.

Benefits oriented to employees' life phases round off the concept for work/life compatibility and show that at Adacor, family-work balance is not an empty slogan, but is anchored in the corporate culture – for the benefit of employees and the company's success.

Additional information:
Compatibility in recruiting:
- Flexible part-time offers at all hierarchical levels
- Job-sharing opportunities
- Flexible interview appointments that take into account childcare times

Compatibility in everyday working life:
- Remote work Options for working remotely
- Core meeting times to plan the workday
- Flexitime/trust-based working hours for more flexibility
- Individual adaptation options for working time models
- Online-first meeting strategy
- Setting up parent-child offices
- Agile work organization for more transparency
- Building parent networks to support

Leadership for family-work balance:
- Clear HR management guidelines for equality and company values
- Leadership guides, coaching and further training for managers in dealing with family-work balance
- Fostering an open and supportive company culture
- Consideration of work/life compatibil ty in target agreements for managers

Compatibility of family and career:
- Access to (online) training opportunities
- Determination of fair assessment criteria for gender-equitable career development
- Individual career paths based on strengths
- Recognition of parental leave as part of personal development

Benefits for work/life compatibility:
- Training internal parent guides
- Monthly subsidy for childcare costs
- Special leave for special events
- Coaching that also covers private topics
- Additional financial benefits such as loans or supplementary insurance

Plan parental leave jointly:
- Structured parental leave process
- Career planning before parental leave
- Further training opportunities during parental leave
- Coaching during parental leave
- Flexible onboarding after parental leave

More information about the author via the QR code:

www.familyvalued.org/Kiki-Radicke-2

Nadine Quosdorf
Founder of #vereinbarkeitjetzt
Germany

Flexible job models for parents in management positions

Abstract
Well, how did it go for you? Did you have a career before the kids and then pick it up again smoothly afterwards? If so, then... congratulations! You are one of the few parents in a leadership position who were able to pick up where they left off after the birth of their children. But you probably had to go back full-time after that, didn't you?

Many of us live in an absolutely equitable relationship before the birth of the first child. We rather naively assume that everything will continue much the same after the child arrives. This is only rarely possible.

Article
The reality after the birth of a child - and the first considerations of what everyday life as a working parent could look like - usually brings us back to old role models: Mom stays at home. "*Dad earns the money*".

Fortunately, these role models usually do not exist in same-sex relationships and a truly equitable decision is more possible. What works for same-sex relationships should also be possible for traditional relationships.

When kids arrive, you will have to deal with two major topics: everyday life as a family, including finances, and returning to work.

Talking about... Expectations

Without knowing you personally, I can guarantee here and now that your life with a child will be very different. Just like your relationship. Not necessarily in the first few years - as a fairly comfortable situation is possible here in Germany thanks to parental leave - but at the latest with daycare or school you will meet a whole new form of organizational challenge. And that's exactly why I can recommend only one thing to you as an absolute basis for a reasonably smooth process as a working mom (or dad): Talk about your expectations! And do it preferably before pregnancy.

- Expectations about how, having children, you want to divide the housework.
- Expectations about who can contribute how much to the joint income, and how much money is needed to make both parents comfortable.
- Expectations about how the topic of pensions can also be managed in parental and part-time work.
- Expectations about how you can remain a happy couple without your own individual lives falling by the wayside.

If you have a clear compass in your private lives, you can also negotiate your return to work more easily. If the topic of leadership and responsibility is important to you, break away from the classic image of part-time or full-time, because there is so much more on offer...

Back to work

The most important advice I can give you when it comes to re-entry is not simply to wait and see what is offered to you. You should know your options. Experience has shown that not everything will go as you were promised when you took parental leave or maternity leave. A stand-in will be found for your position during your parental leave, one of your colleagues will resign or there will be a restructuring. Even if everything looks as if you can simply return to your old slot, you should still look into the alternatives. Perhaps these are more fulfilling after all.

Plan B, C, D...

#1: Self-employment

I have seen a lot of mothers taking a completely new path during parental leave or shortly afterwards: that of self-employment. Be it (as it was for me) because I was bored with the part-time job after all, or because the general conditions (commutes, working hours, daycare place, etc.) make it impossible to resume.

The prospect of self-realization and absolute flexibility is definitely attractive - but be careful: Most of the time, these adventures end in employment or financial dependence after a few years. So, before you decide on this path, be sure to talk to people who have been working independently (and successfully!) for a considerable time, and from whom you can really learn something.

#2: Part-time plus self-employment

I am a big fan of this solution: A job that offers you enough flexibility for your everyday family life, in combination with a "small" self-employment where you can turn your passion into a profession. Which is by no means to say that you should go back to employment just for the money. In the best case you may be lucky enough to work, like me, in an area that is very fulfilling and complements your part-time self-employment too.

#3: Job-Tandem / Job-sharing

The questions of vacation stand-ins and well-thought-out decisions no longer arise in this model. Two people share a job. Not necessarily 50:50, but definitely as equals and, in the best case, with some initial support (JOYntLEADING and TWISE are good addresses here). This is a great solution, especially for ambitious parents who are currently unable to work full-time.

Large companies such as SAP, Beiersdorf or Lufthansa have countless job-sharing models. Why should they let successful and motivated leaders go just because they have to reduce their hours? Unfortunately, still too few companies are asking

themselves this question. Even in times of a shortage of skilled workers and managers and despite extremely high costs for recruiting, the topic is rarely discussed. The large corporations introduced tandems, usually at the request of the workforce. So as always in life, if you don't say what you want, you can't get it!

#4: Part-time plus project leadership

Unfortunately, part-time management positions are still unthinkable for many companies today. Why we cling to hours instead of results remains a mystery to me.

But if there is no other option for you, it is certainly worth thinking about tackling the topic of leadership elsewhere. In private, this can mean volunteering, working for a club/association or for a network. But there are also many possibilities within the company that are not obvious at first glance: New roles and projects that may not even exist today, but that you could get off the ground: How about, for example, setting up a parent network, working in the works council or in health management, taking on (paid) additional tasks such as Scrum/Agile master or healthcare advisor?

Where there's a will... But no matter what you decide in the end, the solution for most of us can be found in the following two concepts: flexibility and trust. And this is absolutely true in both directions: privately and professionally. I cannot simply make demands on the company. The company is also allowed to place expectations on me. And so, for example, it is a matter of course for me that, even if I am officially working only 3 days or 70% of a job, I sometimes take part in appointments on my "off" days; or in return, I can swap one of my "on" days to do something private. "You scratch my back, and I'll scratch yours" applies in all situations.

More information about the author via the QR code:
www.familyvalued.org/Nadine-Quosdorf-2

5 Couple Relationship

Prof. Guy Bodenmann
Clinical psychology
Relationship researcher
Switzerland

Letting partnerships succeed

Abstract

Every person who enters into a relationship wants stability and happiness. The couple's relationship in the family environment has a special responsibility when it comes to the well-being and happiness of all members. In this article, we analyse the most important factors for the stability of that relationship, as well as priorities and how to correct mistakes.

Stability of the couple relationship

When a couple enters into a relationship, they want it to be happy and stable. And what factors promote this stability? In my opinion the main factor is time, i.e. planning sufficient time for maintaining the relationship. In this context, Greek philosophy distinguishes between Chronos and Kairos. Chronos means the quantity of time, Kairos the quality – the aptness of the moment to take time for the other. These are often key to a relationship. In other words, are you there when the other person needs it most? Partners must be sensitive to the need for a conversation in order to

enter into one. This entails being emotionally present when the partner sends such verbal or non-verbal signals. Picking these signals up requires sensitivity and skill.

Another factor is **communication skills**. This includes addressing conflicts in good time. Otherwise, they will become bigger and therefore more difficult to resolve. With the help of this skill, partners can find the right words. The ability to find solutions is also necessary for this, so that small everyday problems can be solved. And thirdly, there is "dyadic coping", i.e. how couples deal with stressful situations together. For example, does my partner respond to my needs or not, and does he/she help me to regulate my emotions or solve specific problems?

And the fourth factor is **commitment**, i.e. the will to "*be with you for a longer period of time*"; in other words, to live a long-term partnership. There are three forms of commitment: emotional, cognitive, and sexual. These are the most important predictors of the stability of a happy relationship.

Priorities in the family

Setting correct priorities is one of the most important tasks of the couple in the family. First of all, there is the maintenance of the couple relationship. Time is limited, so we should manage it well. Good prioritization within family life helps here. The couple relationship begins with the "I", i.e. mothers and fathers alike have to take care of themselves in order not to miss out. Paying attention to one's own "I" - also called self-care - is necessary for a stable relationship. "*In order for me to be a good partner, I have to be doing well too*," could be the resolution. However, this does not mean that I selfishly only pay attention to myself and put my needs first. Partnership always means "we" and thus requires compromise.

Only then do the children come in the list of priorities. If the children come first without restrictions, this endangers the quality and stability of the relationship. The children are then the ones who suffer, i.e. where they should be benefitting, they are the ones who lose out.

In summary, the order is: I, We (couple), children. In most cases, this sequence makes it possible to provide a good basis for the well-being of all. If "I" can no longer do it because of overload and I develop psychological problems, then both the relationships with the partner and the children cannot work.

How can mistakes be remedied?

It is a fact that sometimes desire and reality, i.e. attitude and behaviour, diverge. For example, we want to spend more time with the family, but we don't. How can such a situation be corrected?

First of all, there must be a **reflection** (awareness) of the problematic situation (What is not going well?). Then I need the necessary **motivation**, i.e. the will to get the problem under control. Then the question arises, is the existing motivation sufficient or do I need support?

Once the topic of motivation has been clarified, the third point comes into play: **competencies.** This means: Can I solve the problem? Do I have the necessary skills to do so? Dare I attempt it? I also have to consider the selection of the right opportunity and the "how" of implementation. These are the questions I have to answer here.

If, for example, the behaviour of my partner bothers me, I have to reflect upon why that is. What part does he/she play, and what part do I play in the problem? Where should we start to tackle the problem? Who needs to make what contribution?

Summary

A happy and stable couple's relationship requires time for care, the right priorities and important skills, but also commitment. Family will work if an intact couple's relationship is the foundation.

More information about the author via the QR code:
http://www.familyvalued.org/Guy-Bodenmann-2

Angela Zeidler-Frész
Family trainer, Coach, Author
Germany

How one's own marriage shapes the understanding of family for the next generations

Abstract
Why stay married if everyday married life is such a problem, we asked ourselves during a marriage crisis. Parents not only pass on their genes to their children but also their view of life - what is important and how relationships work. Although other factors are involved, everyday family life in childhood has a lasting impact. We decided to invest in our marital relationship and thus in the relationship skills of future generations: an investment with a high return!

Article
When we married in 1980, we had barely dealt with our own life goals let alone the goals of our marriage. We loved each other; That should be enough - we thought. When a serious crisis loomed after a few years and the marriage threatened to break up, we were forced to think about it. One question arose: Why are we married and why do we want to stay together? Is it worth fighting for our marriage?

We needed a long-term perspective. What would count in 20 and 100 years? What promised the highest "return" on our life investment?

Somewhere I had read that a person acquires a large part of his knowledge before starting school. I was aware that children learn first and foremost by observing and imitating their caregivers - especially social skills, e.g. building stable relationships, finding their own place in social interaction and asserting themselves, being able to speak and argue, being able to endure and solve conflicts. It was also clear to me that during this time the self-image of the person in question is formed, and identity and resilience develop.

So, our children moved up the priority list. They are the politicians, artists, journalists, teachers, influencers, fathers and mothers of tomorrow. As parents, we became aware that what we live in the family today shapes the next generation. And since that generation produces the next one, we also influence future generations. So it is about much more than personal happiness. The task of raising our children gave us a long-term perspective as a married couple, and it demanded the most from us.

Research results have strengthened our convictions.

In their study on how parents influence their children's later relationships behaviour, psychologists Tyler Jamison and Hung Yuan Lo (1) write: "*The people who raise us have a powerful influence on how we understand relationships and which role models we take in our love lives.*"

And the cultural anthropologist, Th. Schirrmacher (2), concludes from an extensive study by Prof. Dan Olweus on violence in Swedish schools: "... *a harmonious, honest and conflict-resolving interaction between the parents is adopted by the children*".

Sociologist Brad Wilcox (3) writes: "*Certainly, many children of unmarried parents develop well. I grew up with a single mother, and I'm doing well. But as a sociologist, I can tell you that, on average, children and communities thrive better when they are rooted in strong families of married parents. Therefore, if you want to save civilization, you should take care of the health of our most important social institution, marriage.*"

When we became aware of how influential our example as a couple was, we became more motivated to invest in our partnership. After all, our children will be the parents of our grandchildren. This change of perspective made us understand marriage as our field of study.

"Sometimes our conversations only revolved around work."

We had conflicts that grew out of our differences. They demanded we learn to negotiate and to find compromises. We have discovered that in every clash there is an opportunity to learn more about each other and to understand each other better. Well-resolved conflicts have rewarded our efforts with deeper emotional closeness. Solutions achieved together and crises overcome have given the relationship depth and stability. We were challenged to deal with the influences on ourselves, our talents, character strengths and weaknesses; and to meet those of our partner with understanding and tolerance. Seeing each other's strengths as enrichment, and being grateful for them, has defused the destructive power of competition and made us more effective as a team.

Sometimes our conversations were only about work. But we are also lovers and best friends, and we want to stay that way. That is why having regular dates is important to us. And we invest in learning more: a marriage seminar or similar is part of the annual program. We have acquired a lot of helpful things over the years. Promptly seeking help in our relationship became as natural as the habit of taking the car in for service when the engine stutters. Sometimes talking to a coach helped us out of a dead end or gave relief to the partner and the relationship when we had stumbled over deeply buried injuries from the past.

During an Internet search on reasons for marriage, I recently found articles on tax-breaks, happiness and men's health at vaterfreuden.de and an article with the telling title: "The partnership of parents as a model for children" (4). This also explains the quality of the parental relationship as a formative factor for the children's later partnerships. After 44 years of marriage, we are now observing in our eight grandchildren how much family influences all areas of life; and we see that our decision has paid off. Investments in marriage pay a high "return" because they shape the future of the next generations.

Literature

(1) Tyler Jamison und Hung Yuan Lo, „Eure Eltern beeinflussen, wie ihr euch in Beziehungen verhaltet – ihr könnt es stoppen", in: Business insider 09.10.2022

(https://www.businessinsider.de/leben/beziehung/wie-eure-eltern-noch-beeinflus-sen-wie-ihr-euch-in-beziehungen-verhaltet-r/).

(2) Dr. Thomas Schirrmacher, „Der Segen von Ehe und Familie", idea-Dokumentation 3/2006, S. 63.

(3) Prof. Brad Wilcox, „Get married: Why Americans Must Defy the Elites, Forge Strong Families, and Save Civilization", in: IFS Institute for Family Studies 20.02.2024 https://ifstudies.org/blog/5-reasons-you-should-get-married (eigene Übersetzung).

(4)   Vaterfreuden.de   (https://www.vaterfreuden.de/partnerschaft/leben-mit-kind/die-partnerschaft-der-eltern-als-Vorbild-f%C3%BCr-die-kinder).

More information about the author via the QR code:

www.familyvalued.org/Angela-Zeidler-Fresz-2

Belinda Brown
Author
Great Britain

The provider role and why it matters

Abstract

As a result of largely feminist ideas, the provider role has received a great deal of opprobrium in the past few decades. In the UK this resulted in a series of policies which strengthened the role of the state and a weakened of the role of the father. The huge increase in fatherlessness is one of its fruits.

The perspective I try to introduce is that the provider role is a very positive thing and is fundamental to our understanding of the father. Being able to provision and care for others is a primary expression of masculinity, which pulls men (and boys) into a reciprocal web of social relationships through which they can take a central place in society, rather than being regarded as anti-social elements to be left on the edge.

Furthermore, once in the family fathers have a distinctive role in the socialisation of children. In a whole range of ways, fathers act as a bridge enabling a child to move from the haven of the mother and home, into taking their place in the wider world.

Article

The provider role has been under attack for four generations. This is because it was understood as the mechanism through which men attempt to dominate and control

women. It was seen as pivotal to patriarchy; the oppression and exploitation of women by men based on the economic 'power' of the husband and father in the home. The hostility towards the provider role led to the state taking an increasingly important role in family life which encouraged a huge increase in fatherlessness. Even where fathers are present, provisioning is devalued, and fathers encouraged to take a more maternal role (1).

Further attack has come from queer theory mainstreamed through the LGBT movement. This has promoted the idea that sex differences are irrelevant both to marriage and parenting. So, fatherhood has taken a further hit. But like motherhood, fatherhood has easily recognisable characteristics. The clearest of these is the provider role. It is the provider role which places fatherhood at the foundation of our humanity and at the cornerstone of the family. It is my intention to explain why here.

"An extraordinarily long childhood, which is only possible through the care of the father".

However, first, we have to be careful about how the provider role is understood. It tends to be understood in terms of a wage packet, but this is a limited understanding. It stems from the industrial revolution which reduced the father to a wage labourer and took him out of the home. But fathers provide many things. Shelter through the building or renovation of houses, social networks for protection or the gathering of resources. Education through imparting the morals of society, or the passing on of their knowledge and skills.

But the provider role goes deeper than that. Fathers as providers have lain at the heart of our embodied existence. This is because compared to other creatures, humans are born prematurely. Human babies cannot remain longer in the womb because our large heads (to store our large brains) would make parturition too difficult. It is only because fathers have been there to protect and provision the mother, that the comparatively premature human baby has been able to survive and thrive.

This is then followed by an exceptionally extended childhood which is only possible because of the father's provisioning. This extended childhood has given us the opportunity to acquire the language, culture, and knowledge which enables us to participate in our enormously complex society (2).

While the providing role of the father was most conspicuous in early human societies, explorations of data reveal how from babyhood to adulthood, the father's social and economic status has played a key role in the mortality rate and opportunities available to the child. What compels men to provision and care for their children? It would appear to be a burden they could easily (and sometimes do) reject. Evolutionary anthropologists have squabbled over this extensively sometimes concluding that provisioning gives the father more mating opportunities and that is why he hangs around.

I would like to propose that the desire to nurture and care for his mate and his children may be more important than opportunities for mating. That men are responsive to the demands and needs of those around them and that this is part of being a man. It is interesting to note, for example, that little boys are more emotionally reactive than little girls (3). Perhaps far from being emotionally stunted, men may have a greater depth of feeling. This would explain why so many love songs and musical opuses are produced by men. Research has suggested that men are more responsive to females, that they are more likely to engage in costly altruism if the target is a female, and that they have greater empathic concern for women than they do for men (4).

This responsive behaviour may blossom into a desire to nurture and care for others as men are tugged into relationships. That having a partner spurs men into productive activity has been amply demonstrated in research. Marriage further increases the male wage premium. Then when men have their own biological children their productivity again goes up. This male productivity strengthens the family. Men's favourable economic circumstances accelerate marriage. They reduce the likelihood of separation or divorce (5).

"Fathers are better able to involve their children in games from an early age."

But providing is important for much more than the resources. Providing is the defining feature of fatherhood on which other behaviours are hinged. It is not the unemployed fathers with time on their hands who are most keen to interact with their children.

Rather it is those who are gainfully employed (6). For far from being a way of gaining status and domination, by becoming a provider a man is symbolically and practically finding himself a place in the processes of reproduction. It is the first step in the transformation of a young male into a potentially responsive and nurturing young man (7).

Once his capacity to provide has helped install a young man in his family, the experience of fatherhood will find him playing an equally distinctive and important role. While the mother nurtures and grows the child within the safe circle of the family, the father will facilitate the child's transition from home and family into the world and adult life.

This happens in a number of ways.

From the earliest ages fathers are better able to engage their children in play. Fathers do more physical, arousing, idiosyncratic, rough and tumble games. They provide their children with novel and complex environments. Through the interaction with objects, people, and the laws of physics, paternal play prepares a child for engagement with the outside world.

"It is fathers who promote the independence of the child the most."

Fathers are more likely to take their children on trips and adventures, bicycle rides and so forth; thus, enabling children to explore their surroundings. By engaging in ball games and sporting activities fathers introduce children to the rule bound universe of competition and set the stage for negotiation with the wider world. The benefits of paternal engagement have emerged in research. These children find it easier to control their behaviour and emotions. They are less likely to display hyperactivity or emotional or behavioural difficulties. They are more able to self-regulate and less likely to get into disagreements at school (8).

As a third member of the family who the child can triangulate with, fathers provide the opportunities to facilitate individuation and start the process through which a child gradually separates from the mother to engage with the outside world.

It is fathers who are most likely to encourage independence insisting that the child make their own sandwiches, tie their own laces and pack their bag for school. Fathers play a particular role in the transmission of religious faith. Fathers provide a sense of security which gives children the confidence to navigate the wider world. The real value of the provider role lies less in the resources which the father brings to the table, although these are important. It is that the provider role gives the man a vital place in the family. Once in the family, the father is the bridge enabling children to eventually leave the family and function successfully in the outside world. Children can do this because their father, has imparted to them hugely valuable qualities, as well as knowledge, empathy, and skills. And the father has ability to do this, maybe as a consequence of his masculinity, but also because of the skills and knowledge he has acquired in the process of practising his provisioning role.

Literature

(1) The erosion of fatherhood is discussed in depth here: https://www.merca-tornet.com/what-is-killing-marriage-and-the-family (last accessed 06/06/2024

(2) This is discussed in some depth here: Brown, B., 2019. From hegemonic to responsive masculinity: The transformative power of the provider role. The Palgrave handbook of male psychology and mental health, pp.183-204.

(3) Tronick, E.Z. and Weinberg, M.K., 1997. Depressed mothers and infants: failure to form dyadic states of consciousness.

(4) FeldmanHall, O., Dalgleish, T., Evans, D., Navrady, L., Tedeschi, E. and Mobbs, D., 2016. Moral chivalry: Gender and harm sensitivity predict costly altruism. Social psychological and personality science, 7(6), pp.542-551.

(5) Wilcox, W.B. and Lerman, R.I., 2014. For richer, for poorer: How family structures economic success in America.

(6) Hofferth, S.L. and Goldscheider, F., 2010. Does change in young men's employment influence fathering? Family Relations, 59(4), pp.479-493.

(7) Dench, G., 2018. Transforming men: Changing patterns of dependency and dominance in gender relations. Routledge.

(8) Amodia-Bidakowska, A., Laverty, C. and Ramchandani, P.G., 2020. Father-child play: A systematic review of its frequency, characteristics and potential impact on children's development. Developmental Review, 57, p.100924.

(9) Andrea Doucet has done a lot of very good work on the role of fathers in childcare for example: Doucet, A., 2018. Do men mother. University of Toronto Press.

Select Bibliography → Links

Brown, B., 2019. From hegemonic to responsive masculinity: The transformative power of the provider role. The Palgrave handbook of male psychology and mental health, pp.183-204.

Brown, B., 2016. From Boys to Men: the place of the provider role in male development. New Male Studies: An International Journal, 5(2), pp.36-57.

Dench, G., 2018. Transforming men: Changing patterns of dependency and dominance in gender relations. Routledge.

Dench, G., 2017. What Women Want: Evidence from British Social Attitudes. Routledge.

More information about the author via the QR code:

www.familyvalued.org/Belinda-Brown-2

Peter Bartning

Alternative practitioner for psychotherapy, couple
and family therapist (DGSF).
Germany

The challenge: to live as a couple

Abstract

Without exception, one's own subconscious chooses one's partner, with the intention
that we mature better and thus become more and more capable of love.
Through the subconscious compulsion to repeat (Sigmund Freud), those themes of
childhood or adolescence that we did not cope with at the time all reappear. And
that is exactly what the couples argue about later, namely about their own, uncon-
scious childhood issues. The challenge is to face your problems in order to heal
them. In this way we can become more and more capable of love.

Article

From the womb onwards our brain records absolutely everything we experience. Most
of it is suppressed into the subconscious – which is why it is so big and influential.
Our subconscious is largely occupied by the so-called Inner Child. This is a symbolic
expression of the child we used to be. And at least in the subconscious, all joys,
longings, wishes, pains, etc. of the Inner Child can slumber, and be awakened, in
adults.

The person we fall in love with is no coincidence. It is always one's own subconscious that chooses potential partners. We live 90% from our subconscious, and only 10% of choices are accessible to our own wanting, planning, and designing. Thus, when we consider that only very few people are familiar with the laws of the subconscious, most couples, sadly, separate far too quickly when a crisis comes along.

Let us take a look at the classic pattern.

You fall in love with each other, the world is rosy, and there is no greater happiness than being together: "Together we are one." You have longed for this love all your life, and now it is here. The Inner Children finally experience themselves as being loved by ideal parents. This time of infatuation is immensely important because it shows what potential lies dormant, subconsciously, in us and in the couple's relationship. After all, these wonderful feelings have been experienced together, and it is this potential that must be developed later, when all seems lost (see below).

Even the best partner will disappoint you sooner or later, and thus the positive feelings of the infatuation phase can collapse completely. Then the Inner Child almost always falls back on old experiences: It closes or at least takes a step back. **You shrink**, so to speak, e.g. you dare not talk to your partner anymore, because the inner child wants to preserve the last remnant of the dreamlike feeling of being in love. In the long run, however, the consequences of this reluctance can be devastating psychosomatic reactions, addictions, an affair, etc. Or one's own children act out the tensions of their parents, e.g. by wetting themselves, failing at school, stealing.

This is usually followed by the **fight phase**: "Right, that's enough!" The partners rebel against each other like pubescent adolescents. In this phase, most couples break up and say prematurely: "Now you're showing your true face!" However, it is almost never recognized that this rebellion is actually directed at the parents or the circumstances at the time. Instead, everything is projected onto the partner. He suffers for no longer taking care of your inner child as a good parent should. Sigmund Freud already observed this "compulsion to repeat", where our subconscious wants to lead us back to heal the wounds of our past, and thus put them behind us once and for all.

However, if it is recognized that the fights usually revolve around trivia (and that essential issues are hidden behind them), this recognition can become the transition to a quieter **negotiation phase**. Alternatively, sometimes the couple is already on the verge of separation, "... but something is still holding us back."

Here it is correctly felt that the subconscious of both partners has not yet reached the goal that it had already shown the couple during the time of their infatuation. But to get to that goal you really need new experiences, because the old strategies of childhood and adolescence only got you so far. You continue to get stuck on the unfinished issues of your own childhood or adolescence, which existed long before the couple's relationship, as in the movie "Groundhog Day". The intention of these repetitions is that the issues finally be healed by us.

And so, a couple's relationship only really begins with the **responsible adulthood** of a mature love, when the couple joins forces to create a life together. Whereas the couple used to face off from two different points of view, during the negotiation, they now stand side by side on a common basis. Now it is no longer the childish love from that longing, subconscious appeal "If you love and care for my inner child, then I will do the same for yours!" Rather, in an adult love, each has already learned to take care of their own. The result is a love without mutual dependence, where one no longer "needs" the other to feel good. This is because, unlike in the infatuation phase's "*Only together are we whole*", you have now experienced *feeling whole and fulfilled with yourself*. So, coupledom includes this challenge: to truly grow up, or come to full maturity, by detoxifying and healing your previously subconscious conflicts. When this happens, you will live less and less in your inner childhood and leave the compulsion to repeat behind you. This is how to achieve and live a lasting love.

More information about the author via the QR code:
www.familyvalued.org/Peter-Bartning-2

Julia Strobel

Coaching for fathers and parents

Germany

Under new auspices – What being a father looks like today

Abstract

The role of the father is undergoing profound and far-reaching changes. The old understanding of the father as the sole breadwinner has become more and more obsolete. It is increasingly being replaced by that of a sensitive team player who actively participates in the lives of his children, takes on housework as a matter of course, and lives in a partnership of equals, eye to eye. All of this has an enormous impact on the father's self-image and the structure of the family. So, what does fatherhood mean today, and what key points mark the new role of "father"?

Article

Introduction

There is a lot going on in the family: old role models no longer fit, new constellations and self-conceptions are emerging. A complex web has emerged between everyday life, work, childcare, providing for the future, social interaction, education and partnership. Fathers are only now finding their new place in it. In short: his role, his duties, his responsibility and his self-image are in flux. What can fatherhood achieve today and what key points mark the newly emerging role of "father"?

Paternity so far

In order to classify these far-reaching changes in all their complexity, we have to see them against the historical background. The father was a successful professional, the sole breadwinner who was mainly responsible for the financial security of the family. "*Fatherhood was nevertheless hardly expressed within in the family, but primarily as a provider for the family. Current research on fathers calls this 'indirect paternal engagement'* [...]" (1). As his counterpart, the mother was responsible for providing of care within the family and for the children. The two-family hemispheres and supposed respective competencies – professionally active vs. emotionally caring – were thus largely separate.

Current development

These assignments and perceived roles are now in flux. The growing women's movement and correspondingly increased employment of women was one of the main initiators of the changes. In addition, there are economic requirements that have demanded new employment constellations. Education and upbringing too are subject to new requirements today. I see the biggest change in the fact that father and mother are increasingly sharing the areas of family life and work equitably and equally. They both feel – and this is new – responsible and competent for both. This is, of course, not true in all regions, social milieus and walks of life; but the trend is clearly established (2).

THE FATHER AS A PARTNER

More and more, fathers are entering new family territory: the emotional area of life and relationships that was previously reserved mainly for mothers. In addition, they have partners at their side who are and want to be well educated, qualified and gainfully employed as a matter of course. Fathers today think more in terms of partnership. This also creates a fundamentally new image of parenthood. It remains a partnership, but an equal one – less hierarchical and more egalitarian, fewer distinct responsibilities and more joint family tasks. Parents today negotiate their life paths between work, career, children and love relationship. They find compromises and try to take everyone's needs into account.

THE PLAYING FATHER

Today's fathers have a genuine interest in their children. They are no longer silent spectators but active companions, supporters, mentors and confidants. Their role is emotionally competent, interested and compassionate. Fathers are an increasingly present part of children's everyday life. Today, the father knows his son's best daycare friend because he takes him to daycare in the morning and spends the afternoon with him twice a week. He knows that his son doesn't like carrots and prefers boiled eggs without the yolk. He helps with homework, puts consolation plasters on grazes, chops fruit for the lunch box, sorts the laundry and cooks dinner. This shared every-day life creates precious memories and promotes mutual understanding – between all family members. For the first time in history, fathers are experiencing themselves as emotionally competent as capable of caring for other people and motivated by the well-being of others.

These changes are new and revolutionary. In my conversations with fathers and parents I experience the uncertainty and helplessness that can arise and overwhelm fathers and mothers alike. But I also see so much genuine and deep interest of fathers in their children, in having a loving and stable partnership, and in real change for themselves, that I am often deeply moved. Trailblazing requires courage, self-confidence, thirst for adventure and perseverance.

Dear fathers, you are indispensable!

Literature

(1) Lieselotte Ahnert: Auf die Väter kommt es an. 2023
(2) BMFSFJ (Hrsg) Väterreport 2021 und 2023., Liselotte Ahnert: Auf die Väter kommt es an, 2023

More information about the author via the QR code:
www.familyvalued.org/Julia-Strobel-2

Excerpt from a lecture by
Prof. Raphael Bonelli
Austria

QR-Code to the lecture

How family works, what helps and what doesn't

Abstract

In this text, we want to discuss what family is and what 'makes it tick'. To describe these, we will use Freud's psychological model of belly, head and heart. This model provides us with the basis for the relationship between the "I" and the "you". The relationship has three levels: Eros, Agape, and Philia. In order for a relationship to be stable, e.g. in marriage, it must include the three levels. The "I" develops into the "you" unless self-love, in the form of narcissism, interferes with this development.

Artikel

Psychological model of the human being

In this text, we want to discuss what family is and what makes it tick.

Let's start with the psychological human model according to Sigmund Freud consisting of head, heart and belly (see Figure 1).

The **belly** seeks the maximization of pleasure and the avoidance of pain. Here are two examples: eating cake ('pleasure') and not wanting to be in pain ('unpleasure'). According to Freud, the belly knows no morality.

In the **head** is the ability to think, i.e. to reason, and to evaluate usefulness.

Decisions are made in the heart. It is at the same time the place of freedom, because the heart can, for example, decide against the suggestion of the belly. The **heart**

decides between good and evil. The values that every person possesses are also anchored in it. This is also the home of the Mosaic law's 10 Commandments.

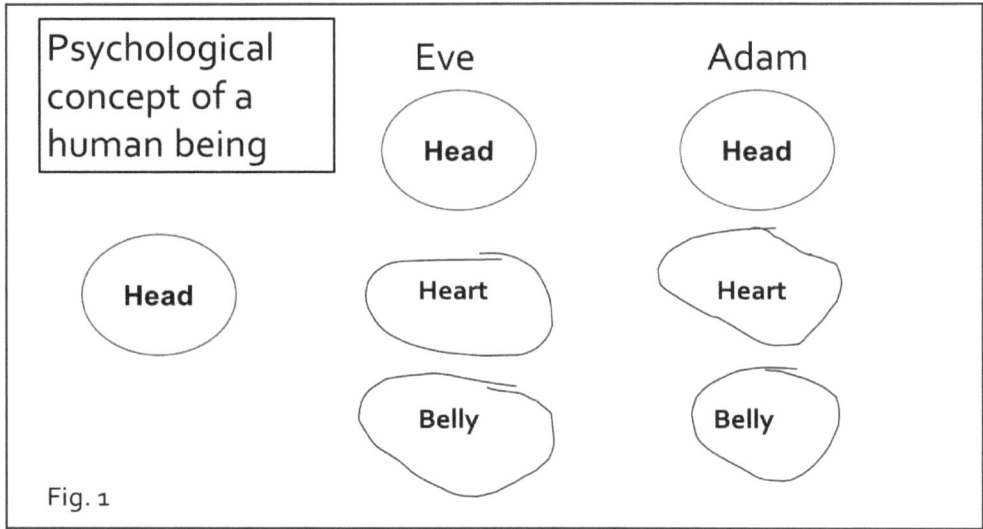

Fig. 1

Relationship between the I and the You

The "I" needs a "you". And, according to Freud, the "I" develops into the "you".

The "I" defines one's own needs. Through the "you", the "I" develops an object relationship. But the libido leads the "I" back to itself. We speak of narcissism whenever the "I" has no interest in the "you". The development of the human being leads from the "I" to the "you" and the "we". This "we" includes, among other things, the family. Moreover, it forms the core of society. The three levels of the relationship between the "I" and the "you" are Eros, Agape, and Philia (Figure 2). And thus, a man can love a woman, or vice versa, on three levels.

In the case of **Eros**, for example, the man would say: "*She looks stunning*". Eros arises from the difference between the sexes. Friendship is formed in **Philia**. Husband and wife talk to each other thanks to Philia. It is an intellectual relationship level. Both of the above-mentioned relationships, Eros and Philia, rarely last for long. It is only through **Agape** that commitment arises: from decision, from engagement. People want a relationship for life, and this can only be achieved through commitment. Eros-based relationships ebb away. They come to an end as soon as Eros wears off. This happens, for example, in old age. Love is thus three-dimensional:

Eros, Agape and Philia. In this form it is stable. Sentences like: "I want a child from you" express the commitment and stability of love. Children are the result of the

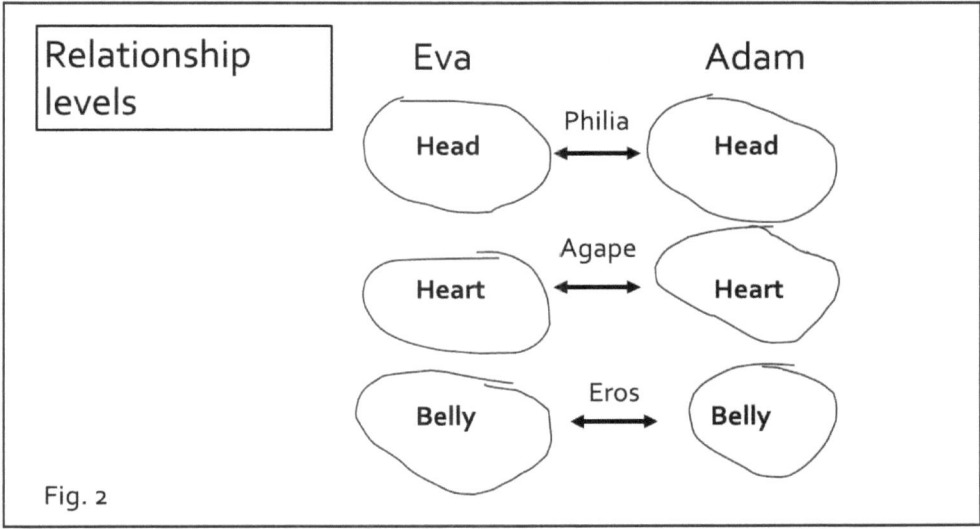

Fig. 2

committed love of parents, and that is how family is created. It is stable if it is underpinned by respectful interaction between the spouses. A loveless joint existence leads to traumatization of marriage and the family.

Let us return to the "I". The human being must free himself from the "I" if he wants to build a stable relationship with the "you". Man is not self-sufficient. He needs the "you". Only through Agape does the "I" develop into "you". We see an example of a false "I" in the hippie generation with its desire for self-realization. There are two negative forms of selfishness that lead to the destruction of the family: narcissism and perfectionism. The narcissist is in love with himself. The perfectionist orbits around himself and seeks the recognition of others. He makes himself dependent on the opinion of others. He wants to please.

Another way of developing into a "you" is through service. From this point of view, work is a service to the other. In contrast, the narcissist works only for himself, for his own self-image. Above we mentioned the hippie generation. It is decidedly ego-

like and overemphasizes Eros, and Eros itself is reduced to self-satisfaction. One consequence of this has been its openness to paedophilia - as in the case of Greens in Germany. Today's zeitgeist seems to be falling into an overemphasis on Eros. The relationship takes place from the point of view of Eros, the maximization of pleasure and its intensification. This then leads to cheating on one's spouse if the spouse does not live up to expectations. I now come to another dimension: freedom through the "you" vs. the lack of freedom through the "I". The perfectionist, for example, just tells people what they want to hear. He/she wants in this way to be liked. This is not service, only a desire to please.

Dimensions of Freedom

Let us now come to Robert Cloninger's concept of freedom. He distinguishes between temperament and character. In his theory temperament is that which is given to us by nature, e.g. being choleric. Character, on the other hand, is what we make of temperament, e.g. a moderate reaction to something. I often hear people say: "*That's just the way I am*!" In my opinion this sentence is stupid, because the speaker assumes they can't or won't change. Anyone can work on himself and change.

We now dive further into the psyche of the human being to see how relationships and family can work. These include the 3 dimensions of freedom:

Inner order
Relatability
Self-transcendence

Thanks to the **inner order** man can discover himself. The three levels of head – heart – belly mentioned above work harmoniously with each other thanks to the inner order. It is said that such a person is at peace with himself, he is with himself.

Thanks to the **relatability** people are open to the "you". With this, the human being moves out of the "I" and into the direction of "you". The problem of man is the overemphasis on the "I". But BF only works if the person is just, i.e. he puts others on the same level as himself. He looks others in the eye. Justice means giving each his due. His due, here, is respect, dignity. These are all virtues. We will see below what other roles virtue plays in our lives. In summary, we can say that the head-heart-belly levels mentioned provide the basis for relatability.

The **Self-transcendence** according to Viktor E. Frankl sets humans free. And the corresponding dimensions of the ST are: The True, the Good and the Beautiful. These correspond to the three levels of head, heart and belly mentioned above. ST means that man rises above himself. It is clear to him that he is serving a cause that transcends him. This service to the true, the good and the beautiful makes people happy and the family free; and that is how relationships work. What corrupts man is a lack of Self-transcendence.

Let us return to the inner order. If this becomes confused, the family topples. I explain the below the correct inner order. God in the first place. He embodies the ideal form of transcendence. In my experience, religious people are happier. Why? Because they have the correct inner order.

In second place the spouse, then the children, then the parents / in-laws and then the siblings. Anyone who violates this hierarchy endangers the stability of the family, hence it no longer "works". One's job takes last place. Anyone who gives his job second or even first priority is looking for gratification. This is a form of ego-centricity. At work you seek self-esteem through the recognition of others. If you define yourself through your job, you are compensating wrongly. You can also compensate wrongly through sports or hobbies.

Personality model		Man	Woman
	Somatic Dimension	Physical and mental strength	Sense of Life and Beauty
	Emotional Dimension	Emotional Stability	Emotional Intelligence / Empathy
	Cognitive Dimension	Systematic Thinking	Social Competence

Fig. 3

A family needs a stable marriage. Therefore, when marriage partners separate it means a catastrophe for the children and for the family as a whole. Once the separation has taken place, the parents seek positive feedback from the children. They seek to please the children; and that too is a form of narcissism. Martin Seligman has developed the connection between happiness and virtue. He comes to the conclusion that the virtues make people happy. He is talking about the virtues of prudence, justice, fortitude and temperance. Coming back to our model: The "I" comes to the "you" through the virtues. But what is a virtue? A virtue is an aptitude for doing good. On the basis of the virtues, we recognize the right thing with the head, we decide for it with the heart, and we strive for it with the belly. We must not forget that children imitate their parents' behaviour, i.e. both their virtues and vices. And so it happens that there are children who instinctively always tell the truth and others who regularly lie. They have trained themselves to behave according to their belly (see diagram above).

Personality model: differences between men and women

Women and men have complementary attributes: characteristics, emotions, competencies, etc. In Figure 3, I have shown the main differences between men and women on the basis of three dimensions. These differences are intended by nature, and not a human construct. The aim of this list is to illustrate the difference between the sexes on the basis of three essential dimensions. Simon Baron-Cohen has dealt scientifically with the difference in personality profiles between men and women. The beauty of these differences between the sexes is that they complement each other, for the benefit of the family.

Some spouses are confused by the difference. My advice is, talk to each other in the spirit of Philia. Get to know your true natures. Since the advent of feminism, there has been a tendency for women to want to score points in masculine areas; and also men who want to be the better mothers. This is anything but sensible.

Studies show that women want a strong man who can also think logically. And men rejoice in the femininity of women. Family only works if the spouses remain true to their roles and exemplify them correctly. Feminism's fight against men overlooks the diversity of profiles and neglects the feminine in women. We are talking about repressed femininity here. But men also sometimes suffer from repressed masculinity. Due to this repression of the feminine and the masculine, parents are no longer authentic, and that poisons family life.

Summary
The family needs self-transcendence so that children can be led to the true, the good and the beautiful, and serve society. If marriage partners respect the head-heart-belly model, then family works!

Link to the lecture: https://www.youtube.com/watch?v=OfSwCXxLlt0

6 Raising children

Susanne Nickel
SPIEGEL bestselling & Speaker
Germany

GenZ – Implications for Families

Abstract

The term "GenZ" has been on everyone's lips for several years. How is GenZ different from previous generations? Young people of the so-called Generation Z have often grown up in a sheltered environment, usually as an only child, or one of two. Sharing, sticking to rules, persistence, taking responsibility for others, supporting siblings – to name just a few aspects, are foreign concepts for many GenZs. In addition, there was often overprotection in education. What should parents do differently today, especially regarding the next generation, Gen Alpha?

Here are some suggestions: Praise only for real performance and for persistence, teaching perseverance, giving age-appropriate responsibilities to the children. Parents should allow children to discover the world through curiosity and to gather their own experiences. But all these measures will only work if they are initiated and supported by love.

Article
Characteristics of GenZ

GenZ includes those born between 1995 and 2010. The term GenZ is mainly used in Western societies because children have grown up there in a secure, even coddled, environment. Many parents of GenZ try to be their child's "best friend", especially in the case of an only child. I call this phenomenon the "Heidi Klum" effect, because she behaves this way towards her daughter. There are mother-daughter relationships of this kind, but also father-son examples. If the children get into such a situation, it is difficult for them later to "cut the cord". School teachers now typically divide parents into certain groups: helicopter parents (they don't let the children out of their sight), curling parents (they remove all difficulties from the children's way), snow ploughs (they take action against the people who could otherwise threaten the children, such as the teacher's grades), tiger parents (they train their children to peak performance) and on top of that, the taxi parents (they take the children everywhere). All these types of parents give children the impression that they are little princes and princesses.

The entry of GenZ into everyday working life

Whereas the parents were there to support the children in the school environment, a cold shock awaits GenZs when they start their working lives. At the beginning of their training, for example, they are often still reliant on their parents. But in everyday working life, parents are not available. Many members of GenZ often lack the maturity even for training: arriving on time, bringing the right documents, concentrating on work for 8 hours, etc. GenZs now need to cope alone, without the helping hand of their parents.

"Parents must manage to impress such concepts as commitment and discipline on their children's lives".

If something overwhelms or doesn't suit them, young people often run away or quit at the first criticism. The phenomenon of "job ghosting" has become rampant in various forms: Either they don't show up for the interview, break off the interview process or fail to turn up on the first day of work, without giving any explanation. The reason is often that they have managed to find a better offer at the last minute. The question arises: why don't young people formally decline the job with their employer? Some studies provide the answer: Many members of GenZ do not have the courage to turn a job down, they find it too unpleasant or lack the necessary communication skills.

This is how employers can deal constructively with GenZ
Members of GenZ are often vulnerable and sensitive. Employers and managers must therefore take the first step and engage with them. Managers need to build a working and appreciative relationship with the GenZ. It is crucially important to establish a personal connection with these young people. Once employers succeed in giving them a kind of home, the bonding will follow. Employers need to draw up a plan for the development of personality and skills. These include competencies such as the ability to handle criticism and to persevere. GenZs need to see a clear purpose for their work, and this must be in line with their own values. Otherwise, it will be difficult to motivate young people in the interests of the company.

"Parents must show steadfastness".

Today's child-rearing needs to be reviewed
Today more than ever, parents must take into account the interests and needs of their children, and to set limits and rules to do so. The strategy of "encourage and challenge" holds good here. Children must be allowed to try things out on their own within the current limits of their freedom. They need to experience for themselves what works and what does not, and not simply take their parents' word for it.

   Parents must be resolute. 'No' remains 'no', even if the child cries, yells or throws a tantrum because of it. Consistency and coherence are required here. Children must learn discipline and pursue goals in a focused manner. The word 'perseverance' needs to be brought back into fashion. The practice of superficial and constant praise for every trivial matter needs to stop! It is better to praise children for persevering and winning through.

Since many families consist of only one child, children need to interact with their peers from other families in order to learn social skills like sharing, thanking, giving, standing one's ground, leading a team, motivating others, etc. GenZ is looking for security, and workplaces are not always secure. Therefore, young people seek security in their families, and these must be a haven for them. The Corona period brought to light the instability of young people. They were prevented from building up resilience at a young age, the way previous generations could. Here, too, the family must be a shelter for them.

Parents must manage to impress such concepts as commitment and discipline on their children's lives. The danger of overestimating one's own abilities is greater today than it used to be. Children need to develop a sense of what is really doable, otherwise setbacks are inevitable. Children have to learn to compromise. You can't have everything you want, whenever and wherever you want it. We need to stop engendering an attitude of entitlement in children.

In Germany, many decades ago, the sense of duty was writ large. Now it has been reduced to almost zero. A revival of this sense needs to be part of the parenting plan. In this way, the children with a good upbringing will become responsible people who can make a difference later on in life. In many families, children help with the housework. This is where a sense of duty and a sense of responsibility can grow together. All the advice above can only bring the desired benefits if it is practised in love. Children and young people are highly attuned to recognizing genuine love.

More information about the author via the QR code:
www.familyvalued.org/Susanne-Nickel-2

Viola Patricia Herrmann
Education Expert
Germany

TRUST, NOT FEAR!
What makes our children strong

Abstract

This text aims to focus on the competencies and abilities of our children. It is intended to encourage parents to hold back at certain points of upbringing, and to replace fear with trust. I would like to strengthen the parents' confidence in their children and give positive impulses for a lovingly less protective upbringing. Possible fears are also addressed, which I can certainly understand as a mother of four children. However, these examples are used to take the children's perspective as well and to convey how they can grow through new challenges. The text is intended to encourage parents not to transfer their own worries onto their children but to give them enough freedom for their individual development and let them experience themselves as competent in dealing with challenging situations. In short: it is a testimony to the greatness of our children, whom we should lovingly encourage rather than suffocate with our own hang-ups.

Article

Recently I overheard a conversation between two neighbourhood boys, both about 10 years old. They were playing football together in the garden at home when one suddenly asked the other: "Hey, what's that you've got hanging on your belt?" "Oh that, that's my AirTag. My mother always puts it on me because she's worried that

I'll get lost otherwise." What the other boy only acknowledged with an astonished look has not left my head to this day. How can it be necessary to track your own child when it is obviously only 50m away? There was also no road between the properties and no other excursion was planned after the game. Unsupervised playtime in a neighbour's garden seems no longer to be as free as it should be.

I have four children myself and I probably know all the fears that we parents go through. We all want our children to have a carefree childhood, protected from the dangers of this world and secure in our love – one that removes all obstacles. That's how it should be, because our children are our greatest treasure. The question, however, is how I deal with my inevitable fears as a parent. The more of them I transfer to my child, the more insecure I make it feel. It gets the feeling that it cannot achieve anything on its own, that it is helpless, and that it has no competence at all. Self-esteem suffers as a result. Personal development, which is fostered by falling down and getting up again, can be inhibited. The child is hampered and may develop a worldview that is characterized by uncertainty and fear. I think that's a pity, and I don't want that for my children.

So how do we control our own fears and set our children free? These five guidelines have helped me to live up to my own standards and strengthen my children's self-esteem in the process:

1.   Creating a safe space

Children must be allowed to try new things, but in a safe environment. On good playgrounds, for example, there are always new challenges that children love to accept and are proud to have mastered on their own.

2.   Avoid excessive warnings

How many times have your parents annoyed you with their warnings? Exactly! A constant "Attention!" or "Watch out!" leads to uncertainty. It is better to stay calm yourself and stand by the child so that he can find a safe way out of the situation himself.

3. **Expand the radius according to age**

Children want to discover new things and try things out. We should allow them this space. Depending on its age, we can gradually increase the area in which our child is allowed to move on its own.

4. **Trust your child**

A very important point that is ignored far too often: our child deserves our trust! We can trust that it is able to act independently and deal with different situations. A powerful "You can do it, I believe in you!" makes children shine and can work inner miracles.

5. **Create your own freedom**

Yes, it's about us parents, because we are the compass for our children. Consequently, we also have to take care of ourselves in order to be able to perform our many tasks well. The older the child gets; the more freedom we can take to try new approaches ourselves. Through our example, our child learns that it is okay to try new things, and that challenges are part of life.

We don't need an invisible leash for our children. We need an invisible bond between us. A bond that consists of love and trust, and that allows both sides - parents and children - the necessary sovereignty for an upbringing without fear. Of course, we must take care of our children, protect them and avoid sources of danger. But we also need to give them courage, confidence and self-esteem in order to overcome life's challenges on their own. The roots that we give them with our love are irreplaceable, and this foundation will carry them throughout their lives. But as our children slowly spread their wings and their wingspans increase, then we must give them more room and support them in their own ways. Here's to a self-determined future full of confidence and free of fear.

More information about the author via the QR code:

www.familyvalued.org/Viola-Patricia-Herrmann-2

Claire de Gatellier

Founder of Famille et Liberté

France

Questions about gender in children and adolescents - What can be done?

Abstract

Children and young adults are in search of their identity. Especially at this time, they need the steadying hand of parents and teachers. And especially at school they are more at risk than anywhere else. In this article I will describe the sexual dangers that lurk for children in schools. In addition, I will provide some tips for the parents, so that they can become that stabilizing and guiding hand for their children.

Article

If we give up, our children will be the first to suffer the consequences. If we question everything in the name of unlimited pseudo-freedom, future adults will be deprived of reliable landmarks and assured facts that are indispensable for the peaceful development of their personality. In schools and in families a hitherto unknown phenomenon is breaking out. Adolescents as well as younger and younger children claim that they no longer recognize themselves in the biological sex in which they were born. In France today, between 1500 and 2000 children are under medical observation in this regard, and there is hardly a school that has been spared from dealing

127

with pupils who demand to be recognised and identified by a different gender than the one assigned to them at birth. This phenomenon is affecting Europe and North America.

"In fact, it is not wise to accept the desire of a child or adolescent for a sex change without thinking."

The fact that adolescents are searching for their own identities, and question their feelings and sexuality, has always been part of growing up. It ends when the young person matures. What is new is the absolute and indisputable nature ascribed to these feelings, and the insistence on blocking the bodily maturation process, and postponing it to a later point in time.

Desire for a sex change is a symptom of deep confusion and great pain that must not be ignored. If one were to take the trouble to look for the real causes of these conditions, one might have a better chance of solving the problem. Unfortunately, the pressure from the LGBT lobbies – which are very well networked in France: in the media, among politicians and in schools – is so strong that the buck stops at the feeling itself, without looking for what is behind it.

Lack of knowledge and due caution along with spurious compassion; our giving in to their subjective desires too quickly and unquestioningly – these are the reasons why young people are being left alone in their pain. This is called the "trans-affirmative" approach, and it has now been made mandatory for all participants by the Education Nationale (Ministry of Education). Lack of knowledge and due caution, we said. In reality it is most unwise to take a child's desire for a sex change at face value, unquestioningly and without understanding what is behind it.

The process of gender swapping
A child or adolescent may go through a period of intense pain and discomfort for family, school, personal, or other reasons. It feels disgusted with itself. So it can happen that he or she thinks that he or she is not in the "right body", and that he or she would be much better off if he or she was not a boy or girl. This is even more so if he or she is being influenced by public debate, by peers from social networks and, unfortunately, sometimes by a doctor. Before allowing a young person to initiate this

anti-natural transformation, one should be fully aware of all the stages and all the consequences.

The first stage is the "social transformation": the first name is changed, and the social environment is informed, the child's appearance, clothing, hairstyle and make-up are changed. Then comes the change in the registry office.

All this would not be so bad, and the adolescent would still be able reconsider, were it not for the pressure to continue playing the game that is exerted by the opinions of others: social networks and the influence of LGBT networks. Over time, the return to the original, innate identity becomes more and more difficult. Nevertheless, it would still be possible.

However, at the same time as the social transformation come chemical puberty blockers, which can be prescribed from the age of 10. They are supposed to delay puberty so that the person concerned has more time to think it over. But in this area, it is no longer so easy to undo everything, emphasizes Dr. Anne-Laure Boch [1], neurosurgeon at the Pitié-Salpetriere hospital in Paris. The unity of the human person does not allow a clean separation between the psychological and the morphological. If sexual development is delayed, psychological and morphological delays follow, and these cannot always be remedied.

From the age of 15, the medical conversion is allowed to begin, i.e. the girls receive male and the boys female hormones. If the adolescent persists, surgery can be performed. First comes the removal of the respective genitals, then their "reconstruction". In principle this procedure is reserved in France for adults only, but it is sometimes performed on younger people. The youngest patient to have her breasts removed at Robert Debré Hospital was 14 years old. In both cases, both drug and surgical conversion therapy, the patient was originally perfectly healthy. From this point onwards, at the latest, the patient becomes dependent on severe medical therapies for the rest of their life.

In addition, they will have to endure serious side effects for the foreseeable future. The artificially crafted genitals never function properly: they allow neither sexual pleasure nor reproduction. It must be made clear to everyone that this debilitating path can only change the appearance, the "perceived" gender, but never its essence, because gender is in fact indelibly inscribed in the genes of every human being.

"After the first sex change, the child and his family may realize that the first sex change was not the true solution to the problem."

Is it right to acquiesce to a child's desire, and to leave it to make such a momentous decision alone, the consequences of which it is unable to grasp at that age? We cannot pretend we are fulfilling our duty to the child's well-being by acquiescing or possibly even promoting it. The pain of a child leading to such an extreme desire is enormous. The first duty is to take him seriously, to listen to him and to investigate together with him what the underlying causes of his desire really are. The child sincerely believes that the only relief from his distress lies in sex reassignment.

In reality, the cause is very likely to lie elsewhere. Simply failing to carry out further investigation and being content instead to take the quick way out through a sex change, is tantamount to "failure to render assistance to a person in need". This is due on the one hand to the damage to the physical and mental health caused by the above-mentioned procedure, and on the other hand because the true cause of this child's distress was not discovered and therefore not treated. So, it is very likely that after the initial euphoria, the real problem will come to light with even more force.

This is testified by more and more "detransitioners", who are now speaking out publicly in countries where sex reassignment has been practiced for some time: Sweden, Norway, the United Kingdom, and the United States. Ms. Lisa Littman has published a study on detransitioners in Sweden. She points out that a third of them were persuaded to do so by a third party. Some examples:

- Over time, they realize that gender is an immutable fact
- The transformation has not solved any of the original problems
- They regret that they were not counselled into the proper treatment of their real problems
- "In a world where I have no place neither as a man nor as a woman, I find myself squeezed between the two sexes."

In the face of these experiences, the countries that started this practice are beginning to change their jurisdiction and adopt new laws that severely restrict the transitioning of minors, even going so far as to close the clinics involved, such as Tavistock in London, which was a veritable "*trans-factory*". But in other countries, such as France, we are still in the boom phase.

What can parents do?

How can we avoid this happening, even if it does reach a point where our child wants a sex change?

Prevention is better than cure:

1) Computers with social networks should be avoided at all costs, even if they are hard to avoid.

They prevent children from developing an independent and stable personality because they promote only imitation. The children are no longer themselves. They get absorbed into a group that has its own rites and rules. Concern for their own image (number of "likes") replaces their inner lives and pulls them away from their family and surroundings into an unreal world. They distance themselves from reality and from nature as it really is and see only a dream world. But the teachers themselves always use digital media, if only to assign homework. This is very worrying.

2) Children must be kept away from pornography at all costs, because it gives a derogatory image of the woman, who always consents to sex, and also of the man, who consists only of his erection. This can only lead eventually to disgust for one's own body

3) Father and mother must always keep very close to their children. Don't tell children, "We can talk to each other from such and such a time to such and such a time ". Do as much as possible together: walk the dog, watch the soccer game, make jam, play cards, be interested in the content of the homework and not just the grades. All this time off the computer will anchor our children in reality and instil confidence in them. Psychiatrists and psychologists agree that the desire for sex reassignment often lies in the inability to identify with the father or mother.

4) Playing sports, physical exercise, hiking, bike rides etc. that promote the simultaneous development of body and mind and sharpen a sense of the body's own intrinsic laws.

5) Contrary to modern fads in upbringing, the child must learn very early on that it is not omnipotent, and not the centre of the universe. It did not create itself, and it should accept life, its sexual body, as a gift and not as a personal conquest.

Laws exist, not only civil laws but also the laws of nature, and without them we lack a solid trellis upon which we can grow.

"Parents should separate the at-risk young people from their false friends on social media, in their school class or in the clique."

And if your child is already asking for a sex change?
Don't panic. Do not lose sight of the wood for the trees.
1)   Accept and understand that the desire for transformation is only a symptom and not necessarily the solution.
2)   Dr. Christian Flavigny [2] - paedopsychologist and psychoanalyst - says: "The child is not in the wrong body, it just feels incapable of inhabiting the body it has. Before resorting to the irreparable remedy of sex change, it is necessary to find out why this is so.
3)   Mrs. Rita de Roucy [3] - clinical psychologist and psychotherapist - notes 3 very common causes: The child was a victim of sexual abuse - recently or long ago. In the case of a girl, it is a defence mechanism. "If I'm not a girl, this can't happen to me anymore." In the case of a boy, it is the fear that he will later be driven to inflict on someone else the shame he has experienced himself.

"Let's not leave our children to those who give them false hopes".

But also:
- the attitude of parents who would really have preferred a child of the opposite sex.
- a bad image of the same-sex parent.
- pornography experienced, and sexual experiences that devalue the body. To discern true causes you need professional help, but please get the right help.
4)   Extract the adolescent from their false friends on social networks, from their class or their usual peer group. If a young person has "come out" to his friends as a "trans", then the loss of face will be hard to bear. It will be difficult to resist the pressure. Changing schools can be helpful.

5) Get back to reality as much as possible: cultivate closeness to nature, the ability to appreciate things, to be amazed, to be surprised, to do sports, to go for a walk, to hike (if possible, in another region, as this brings some variety). Reading or listening to books, watching documentaries and not just fantasy fiction, that is, media that show real people overcoming real obstacles; people that are themselves inspiring role models.

6) But above all, show the child a lot of patience and gentleness, that you love him/her, that you are proud of him/her, that you understand his/her suffering, that you are on his/her side. This has nothing to do with the allowing the child to get away with anything.

Let us not abandon our children to the illusion peddlers. The best antidote is the family, the hearth of life, which offers the child a safe and harmonious place where he experiences love and connection, finds his place so that he can also find him in society. A society that renounces the value and stability of the family becomes a broken society from which children themselves become unstable, unhappy and irresponsible adults. That does not need to happen. Many young people long for family commitment and loyalty.

Literature

[1] Dr. Anne-Laure Boch, neurosurgeon at the Pitié-Salpêtrière Hospital, Paris
[2] Dr. Christian Flavigny, child psychiatrist and psychoanalyst
[3] Rita de Roucy, Clinical Psychologist, Psychotherapist
[4] Lisa Littmann, US Professor of Gender Issues. Study: *Sudden-onset gender dysphoria in adolescents and young adults: a descriptive study*

More information about the author via the QR code:
www.familyvalued.org/Claire-de-Gatellier-2

Hedwig von Beverfoerde

Action for Marriage & Family
Germany

Does the family have a future? - The Greatest Challenges for today's family politics

Abstract

One would think that no state could function without the family. It is here that relationship bonds are lived, children are raised, loved and strengthened for life – indispensably and free of charge. The protection of the family should be absolute priority. Instead, the family sees its very foundations, man and woman, threatened by government plans – currently by the "Self-Determination Act" and a new law on lineage and parentage. To secure the future of the family we need a political transformation.

Article

Loved or hated, longed for or rejected and all shades in between – the family leaves no one indifferent. It is the human bond that connects the past, present and future, happiness and destiny at the same time. Over the centuries it has propagated itself through physical and spiritual bonds. Born into a family, it is there that we discover our identities, so we can decide later for ourselves whether and whom we marry, have children and thus start and continue a family of our own.

Once founded, the family has the potential to become a power plant. Every day, the family provides educational services that are not only free of charge, but above

all indispensable. From mother and father, grandparents and siblings, within the good old family, the child learns to play, speak and walk. It listens to fairy tales, stories and songs, takes on its first responsibilities, practises virtues, acquires social skills and morals and develops its own independent character. Whether it is the school, university or employer – all of them can only build on the basic preparatory work of the family, and no one can replace it. Not only the children benefit, but also friends, neighbours, the elderly and the sick experience helpfulness, care and support through the family.

"Let's help our society rethink. Let us draw attention to the value and beauty of marriage and family through our words and examples."

It should therefore be a matter of course for the state, society and the economy to put the protection of the family first and foremost. But in reality, we are experiencing the complete opposite in Germany today: many people can barely afford to start a family anymore or can no longer imagine doing so in the face of growing fears about the future. Fathers are ridiculed in the media and pop culture, and mothers who are not employed because they are taking care of their children are considered a loss to the economy. Children are already sexualized, politicized and played off against their parents in day-care and school. The legislature redefines marriage and family at will, and the Ministry for Family primarily promotes lobby groups for sexual minorities.

In Germany an absurd "Self-Determination Act" aims to undermine the natural identity of man and woman – the very cornerstones of the family. Next the government plans to completely revise parentage and family law and legalize egg donation and inhuman surrogacy - both direct attacks on the nature of the family, with unforeseeable legal consequences. In schools and day-care centres, children are exposed to a shameless "sex education of diversity".

It is high time for change. The family always has a future, because it is the future. But this future will not take care of itself. Due to its many powerful opponents, the family needs friends, supporters and defenders. It is all about achieving real political change for the family. A few family-friendly concessions are not enough. The family should be the model for the state and society. All decisions in politics, administration, business, education, research, etc. must take into account the well-being of the family. Freedom and the spiritual and material well-being of families are, after all, crucial for the future of any country.

Let us help our society to rethink. Let us draw attention to the value and beauty of marriage and family through our words and example. Let's show that a healthy, happy family is possible. In this way, we reawaken deep-felt longings and shape a common awareness of the good, the true and the beautiful.

Let us stand up resolutely for tax and social security reform to ease the burden on families and, at the same time, insist on the parents' natural right to raise their own children. Let us confidently campaign for an end to the propagation and financial support of "alternative family models" and the social experiments of the "progressives".

This is best achieved within the framework of a broad family movement – together with other vigilant people who raise awareness within their personal environments, who advocate for the rights of marriage and family in schools, associations, church congregations and at the workplace. The family needs courageous people who call or visit members of parliament and, if necessary, take to the streets and protest publicly. Even a small effort can make a big difference. What are we waiting for?

More information about the author via the QR code:
www.familyvalued.org/Hedwig-von-Beverfoerde-2

Leni Kesselstatt

Head of Familien Allianz
Austria

"Tell the children about love" - How to protect children from ideologies

Abstract

We founded the "*Familien Allianz*" a little more than 10 years ago to inform parents about family-related topics. We provide arguments for the socio-political debate and for decisions and support parents in their child-rearing duties in the light of the Christian view of mankind.

Our experience shows that the ideological pressure on children is constantly increasing, more and more often they are confronted with things that unsettle, confuse and sometimes cause lasting distress. Who but us parents have the duty to protect them from this?

Article

We founded the "*Familien Allianz*" a little more than 10 years ago to inform parents about family-related topics. Parents can find us on our homepage www.sexualerziehung.at. They contact us because they want to know which questions they should ask at parents' evenings or at teacher meetings, or what background information is important in order to be able to better assess the topic. Often the information comes too late – their child has come home distraught, and parents do not know what happened at school.

Since ideology most often affects all topics of the body, i.e. human sexuality and, by association, human identity, our advice is this: Explain the facts of life to your child before someone else does! Once children are armed with this knowledge, much of what is aimed at them from the outside bounces off. We parents can sensitize our children lovingly and with the help of precise language. All too often today, the Internet with its crude and pornographic content takes over this task and thus leaves marks of disgust and shame on a child's initial experiences. To avoid this, parents should use the privilege of being the first to provide initial information as a trump card to bring their children closer to the unique and beautiful nature of the transmission of life.

"Make alliances with other parents".

Some parents have never heard the facts of life properly explained themselves, and so lack the appropriate language for it, or feel insecure about this topic. We help parents with selected books and material on the websites, which we have checked ourselves. These materials support parents in discussing the complex topic in an understandable and child-friendly way. The child will therefore also choose us parents as its preferred source later on, when it has questions. Whenever children begin to search for answers on their own, they inevitably come across distressing, pornographic content.

In addition to explaining the facts of life to the children, it is important to get a regular overview of the teaching materials, to leaf through books occasionally and to discuss them with your own child. If you come across unsettling content, for example in brochures distributed at your child's school, then talk to your child about it and clearly 'call a spade a spade', such as, "Only a man and a woman together can make babies."

At the beginning of school, we advise parents to seek election as class representatives. This will probably give you a better idea of what is planned and allow you to react quickly. Form alliances with other parents. It is always better to go to the school director in groups than alone! If a parents' evening on the topic of sex education or abuse prevention is scheduled, please ask what materials are used (names of the books or films) and have them show these to you. You have a right to know! Almost all content from external workshops or materials used by teachers is based on the presumption that the child is a "sexual being" and should be stimulated proactively at an early stage. Even if speakers seem very understanding and have adopted "our" language, remember that teachers are usually sent out of the classroom, the classroom door closes and the children are caught off guard by the Q&A session, where students can ask anything, they want to know. This is the time where inappropriate expressions and matters of adult sexuality are very likely to be brought up. Sometimes children are even told that they are not allowed to talk to anyone about it, as numerous reports from parents and children have shown.

However, if you are already talking to your child; if your children are informed by you about the biological changes in their bodies, then they will turn to you first with any questions or confusion they may have. It is through conversation within the family that the child recognizes the true value and beauty of sexuality. It gets to know and appreciate its parents as competent, understanding and enlightened people to whom it can turn with confidence even in difficult situations, such as in the case of an unplanned pregnancy. Protection of life begins in the family!

More information about the author via the QR code:
www.familyvalued.org/Leni-Kesselstatt-2

Esther Bockwyt
Psychologist
Germany

Raising children in a woke environment

Abstract

Families are responsible for raising their own children. What do they do when they are confronted with an ideology that says, for example, that gender is only a sociological construct? The solution for parents is: information about the conditions in daycare centres and schools, and preventive measures through authentic sex education.

Article

What do we mean by woke

A new ideology is spreading in Western societies. Its name: "Woke". It divides those who have recognized it into its advocates and opponents. Conflicts and alienation are the result. This ideology lays claim to certain topics with positive connotations such as justice, diversity or anti-racism. This ideology leads to a worldview, and it is no small matter. Woke has the potential to influence the future of modern democratic society. This is due to its radical demand for change, with sometimes totalitarian excesses. It was created about 30 years ago in the academic environment of US universities and has become firmly established a l over the world thanks to journalists, activists and donors. Media, led by X and Instagram influencers, have more or less consciously adopted woke thought, and thus made it socially acceptable.

Companies have discovered "wokeness" as a marketing tool for themselves. And they expect customers to approve of this. And so it happens that the destructive nature of woke ideology remains hidden. As a result, parallels to other totalitarian movements in human history are no longer drawn.

Almost unnoticed, wokeness has become an ideology that apparently can no longer be refused. An ever-increasing social pressure constricts people like hardly anything seen before, and at the same time renders impossible any voluntary woke attitude from within.

Woke movement originates from feminism

The philosopher Judith Buttler, professor of rhetoric and comparative literature at Berkeley, started with a feminist movement, then moved on to the topic of "gender as a construct", into the queer movement. Initially around 1930, Woke was about racism against blacks. Then it was expanded to include diversity. The character of activism has always been preserved.

Children and adolescents are affected by woke

From the above, one could get the impression that it is a movement by adults for adults – far from it! Children in institutions such as daycare centres and schools are increasingly confronted with woke in our country, because the activists of this ideology have brought concrete measures into these very institutions. What do these measures look like? The children are sometimes told that biological sex is a construct, and that people are born gender-neutral, as per Buttler's theory. Thus, children are allowed to choose their own gender. As a result of the rising influence of "gender theories", many sex-change operations have been carried out on children and adolescents, the aftermaths of which have already led to the closure of a hospital specializing in these measures in England, for example. The sex-changing measures range from puberty blockers to hormone treatment to surgery and have been widely criticized for their massive interventions in developing bodies. If woke activists continue to influence the curricula in some schools in their favour, sex education will be increasingly driven by woke rules and ideology. Occasionally one heard of "body exploration rooms" for small children. Increasingly, one gets the impression that the aim and implementation is to confront younger and younger children with the topic of sexuality.

Children talking to their parents
The practices described above can destabilize children. Many dare not talk to their parents about what they have experienced. They feel ashamed.

Rather, it is the parents who notice unusual behaviour in the children and then ask them why. Parents may then be shocked and feel betrayed by the school or daycare centre.

Preventive measures taken by parents
Parents are now needed as never before. If they notice that children are confronted with inappropriate or incorrect information about gender and sexuality in institutions, it helps to show the child a different point of view. In addition, it may make sense to approach those daycare centres and schools in person, in order to prevent further abuse. When parents do this, they are likely to be confronted by daycare supervisors or school teachers who can try to make them feel guilty for not raising their children "correctly". Parents are advised to react confidently and constructively - for their child's sake.

Woke everywhere
Woke is - it can be said – everywhere: in daycare centres and schools, but also in universities, in government offices and at many companies. The woke 'virus' is spread under the guise of diversity. It often restricts freedom of expression too: more and more often, lectures by scientists who are critical of the woke are obstructed or made impossible by woke activists, with the accusations of "misanthropy", "transphobia", "racism" and so on. This is "Cancel Culture" in its purest form!

What families can do
Woke affects the entire life cycle. Therefore, families must be on their guard in all areas of life in order to be able to counteract it, and to do so preventively.

For this purpose, please refer to the articles in this book by Leni Kesselstatt and Hedwig von Beverfoerde.

More information about the author via the QR code:

www.familyvalued.org/Esther-Bockwyt-2

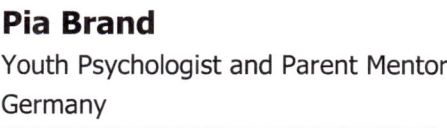

Pia Brand
Youth Psychologist and Parent Mentor
Germany

"I'm turning off the router on the count of three" - How can 'Digital Natives' learn media literacy?

Abstract

As a psychologist and mentor for parents of pubescent kids, I cannot avoid the topic of using online media. They are omnipresent and seem to be THE bone of contention in almost every family. Yet most parents like to use online media themselves ... just differently! I see exactly this as one of the most important educational tasks of today: teaching media literacy. In my opinion it will not succeed through bans, router wars and rigid media times; but rather through relationships, meaningful interaction and the offering of an alternative, attractive world quite apart from Instagram, TikTok and gaming.

Article
According to Statista, the average screen time of 13-18-year-olds is 25 hours per week. This is more than a part-time job. Naturally, parents are worried, and it is not surprising that there are frequent arguments within the family on this point.

But if we take a more nuanced look at the use, what is consumed, when and how integrated the media are into the real world, it quickly becomes clear that the issue is very complex. Simple bans and parental prohibitions will not achieve the goal we want for our young people: media literacy!

Our teenager's brain is constantly evolving. However, since development is not always uniform, and not linear, we are concentrating in particular on the growth of the areas that we often need: Language, motor skills and social interaction do not develop as well under increased screen use. It makes the world beyond the screen seem much more complex, and the young people find it harder to keep up with it. We observe that the control of impulses in particular is significantly reduced. This often leads to extreme outbursts of emotion, which often frighten the young people themselves. They hardly recognize themselves and then withdraw (partly out of shame) back into the online world that they are familiar with.

Young people need a safe environment, and solid relationships, before they dare to step out into the outside world. With all the changes they have gone through, with all the challenges and tasks that come with growing up, they have to feel that they are important to us. The pressure on young people is extremely high. That is why it is all the more important to teach teens to find a healthy life/screen balance. **After all, just because they are "digital natives", and thus familiar with the online world, that doesn't mean that they can find a healthy way to handle it on their own. This is where we as parents come in.**

Each family has to make its own rules and also customize them for each child. It is important that media literacy is about accompanying the children, from (a) guided use regulated by us to (b) competent, self-confident and, above all, safe solo use.

On the way there it is important to remain open. If we make too many regulations, it quickly leads to young people taking us less seriously as we get older. And we unintentionally limit the possibility of their exercising their own self-discipline. As is so often the case, it is advisable to first look at our own usage behaviour. Do I have a healthy relationship with my phone? Do I consciously take time offline? Do I prioritize face-to-face over digital interaction? When we prefer for ourselves physical presence and undivided attention, we allow our young people to experience how good this real contact feels. The immediate effect is improved inner well-being, which reduces the feelings of stress and loneliness. According to a survey by Statista in 2022, 55% of young people often or always feel lonely; and that despite the impression that we're in contact with others constantly. Let us remember how exciting we found online media as children: Gameboy until late at night or playing Snake on our parents' cell phones. Constant use of online media is extremely appealing, especially to children and young people. And today those online media are omnipresent, and even more deeply interwoven into our everyday lives, because we can take almost everything with us everywhere. Pubescent youth feel a great need to try things out, to put themselves on display and, above all, to belong. For all of this the online world offers many opportunities and pedestals. What is the need currently driving the adolescent? And how can we perhaps satisfy this need in the real world?

Is my child longing to preen and be seen right now? Longing for recognition? For interaction? Or is there simply a desire for distraction from heavy topics? What is it that my child really needs right now, and how can I help him to judge what best satisfies that need at this moment? When confronted with nothing but prohibitions our young people do not gain the understanding of values and social competence that we hope for them. To get through to them it is more helpful to answer the questions: Why is it worth putting your mobile phone aside? What do I want to do during this time instead? And with whom? As is often the case, so with media literacy: to achieve a healthy balance the focus needs to be on relationships, meaningful interaction and an attractive world away from digital media.

More information about the author via the QR code:
www.familyvalued.org/Pia-Brand-2

Dr. Karl-Maria de Molina
Entrepreneur, Author, Lecturer
Germany

Parents need skills for raising children

Abstract
In the world of work, it is common to describe job roles based on the skills required for them. Parents also have a job role: "parenthood". What does the corresponding job profile look like, i.e. what skills are necessary for the role of "parenthood"? Based on the skills known from the world of work, we will draw up a list and comment on it.

Article
Before the birth of the child, many parents already have a clear idea of what role the child can / should play in life. Actors like Michael Douglas, racing drivers like Mick Schumacher, politicians like Monika (Strauss) Hohlmeier are descendants of parents with similar professional profiles. The German saying, "the apple doesn't fall far from the tree" is confirmed - at least sometimes, by experience. A new study by the University of Vechta (see scinexx.de link below) confirms that parents have a very strong influence on the child's capacity for scientific thinking. This stems from their attitudes

towards knowledge and education. Thus, according to the study, parents exert a stronger influence than school.

Parents consciously or unconsciously wish to leave an impression on their children's lives - be it in the choice of profession, values, ways of behaving and speaking, position in society, etc. The content of this impression or upbringing is quite different, depending on the parents' view of humanity. No household pins such a plan to the wall, rather it arises unconsciously. And yet, in order to convey this impression, parents need qualities and competencies in addition to virtues and values. Today we will focus on the former.

As part of my work as a personnel diagnostician I deal with the following question on a daily basis: Which competencies and characteristics are necessary for a certain job role? The "job role" we want to look at today is called parenthood. Needless to say, these competencies are clearly of lower priority than virtues such as love, devotion, understanding of others, etc. After that come such values as consideration for others, justice, solidarity, etc. and only then come the skills. In our company, we have built up a catalogue of over 200 competencies. These are drawn from many studies by well-known institutions. I list below some of the competencies from the catalogue and justify their necessity for the job role of "parenthood". It is a small selection of approximately 60 competencies necessary for life.

#1: Communication in connection with conflict-resolution skills: Communication between parents and a child takes place in a manner appropriate to the child's age. In most cases, children must be able to understand the decisions of their parents in order to obey them. Even with good communication, tensions and conflicts within the family are inevitable. Mediating conflicts, and leading them to a consensus, is crucial for building a stable parent-child relationship. Reducing excessive tension to a tolerable level requires a high degree of communication and conflict management.

#2: Empathy and patience: Children need to feel understood. This requires parents to exercise patience and show empathy. Parents are much more than just teachers for the children: they are their "upbringers" for life. Upbringing means giving what is necessary and demanding what is owed. In addition, empathy is necessary in order to recognize children's needs; then patience is required to endure the mistakes.

#3: Consistency: Upbringing requires continuity in the specifications and in the focus on the goal. What was true yesterday is still true today. We could also call it straightforwardness. The opposite confuses children because they don't know which requirements still apply today and which no longer apply. This severely disturbs children. Prof. Michael Schulte-Markwort confirms this thesis. Incidentally, he is one of the authors of this book.

#4: Problem-solving skills: Problems occur constantly in the family environment, e.g. grandparents suddenly fall ill, the car won't start, the basement is flooded, the trains are on strike, the daycare centre is closed today - the list could be continued indefinitely. Parents - with the help of the children - must be able to resolve all these events into a more or less positive outcome.

#5: Structure and discipline: A household needs a flexible and clear structure so that (as far as possible) everything runs smoothly: getting up on time, having breakfast, taking children to school, driving to the office, etc. Parents must provide this structure and - very importantly - exemplify it. Structure provides security and predictability for the children, so that they know where they stand.

#6: Flexibility: The above structure, and also discipline, need to be adapted to changing circumstances. Therefore, flexibility complements structure and discipline. The three competencies belong together. Balancing them is doubtless a question of skill.

#7: Emotional intelligence: What reaction is appropriate to a specific event? This is what our emotional intelligence tells us. It regulates and adapts our reactions to produce the optimal effect. Children behave differently from adults. Let us say they smash a valuable vase, for example. Thanks to emotional intelligence, we evaluate the event and think about how we should react to it. Those who fly into a rage reveal a blatant lack of emotional intelligence. Such behaviour can destroy any relationship

with children. Thanks to emotional intelligence, even a choleric person can react appropriately - or at least apologize afterwards.

#8: Mentoring: In the studies on children's academic success, one important factor always comes to light: the level of education of the parents. Among other things, they are mentors for the children's professional development. The choice of vocabulary, of conversation topics for the table, of television programs provide a foundation for their status in society and create a "calling card" for their entry into professional and private life.

#9: Self-control: In point #5 we talked about structure and discipline. In order to achieve this, parents must be able to control themselves, i.e. to do what the situation requires and not "let themselves down" or postpone issues without good reason. Self-control requires willpower, which varies greatly in us humans. Some have a lot, others less. Without self-control, many tasks cannot be solved at all because they require perseverance. Raising children is one of them. Parents need "staying power".

Summary
We need many of the aforementioned skills for our professions. The application of these skills to the family environment clearly requires adaptation. We all have the competencies listed above. The only question is, do we have them in the correct form and in sufficient quantities to manage a family household? With this article I hope to have sensitized you, dear reader, to a topic that we rarely have on our "radar screens", and one that can lead to discord in the family if disregarded.

More information about the author via the QR code:
www.familyvalued.org/Karl-Maria-de-Molina-2

Luis Daniel González

Author and blogger
Spain

Some suggestions to teach children the beauty of reading

Abstract

The following lines contain some pointers for parents and educators who want their children and students to become good readers. With these premises, which in my opinion form an intellectual framework, we can provide some guidance for evaluating the content of children's and young people's books.

Article

Considerations

1)   Chesterton said that "literature is a luxury, but fiction is a necessity." We all need stories of all kinds, but unfortunately many have not learned to appreciate literature to a sufficient extent. Since children and young people are primarily looking for stories that speak to them, reading and literary education must above all aim to enable them to distinguish which stories are valuable and which are not, so that they can find good literature on that basis.

2)   A second consideration for educators is that they should compile a list of the best books, and especially the best works for children and young people, past and present. Although it is not possible for them to know all these works, it is possible that they have read many of them, since quality is better than quantity. Then the educators must try to adapt the selection to the circumstances and conditions of the

readers. In this task of educators, it makes sense that they value books for what only books can give us, and not for what other types of narration, such as podcasts or videos, can better convey to us.

How to promote reading

3)	"What eyes do not see; the heart does not feel" is a well-known Spanish proverb. Books, and especially picture books, are very important for building good reading habits in children. When it comes to books, the "showcase effect", i.e. their proximity and availability, is crucial. Well-presented products sell better; and keeping an eye on them always opens up new possibilities for discovery or rediscovery. For children it is not the same to grow up in a house where there are no books within their reach, and with parents whom they never see reading, as it is to grow up in a house where there are dozens of attractive books, with parents who love to read and to talk regularly about the books that they have read.

4)	It is necessary to find out the books that are appreciated by the children. Even if they are not the most valuable in all aspects, they tell us a lot about the needs of children as well as their deficits in reading skills. It is a matter of using these clues. There are stories that can serve to stimulate reading skills, stimulate the imagination and build a bridge to better works. This is especially true if there is someone to help the reader distinguish between what has quality and what doesn't.

5)	Parents should know first-hand what stories their children are reading and then read those stories to them. Reading the very books that children read is some-thing so important that you have to do it, even if you are not a good reader yourself. Parents must approach the fictions that their children enjoy in a similar way to the way they get to know their own friends and acquaintances. Some are suitable for a good conversation, others less so, and others are a support for life.

6)	In summary, it is important to find out the reasons why young readers prefer some stories to others, even if adults cannot relate to those reasons themselves. Adults should find out the reasons behind these preferences. It all depends on the content, form or tone of the language. From this, insights can be gained about the emotional needs of readers and the state of their reading ability.

How to rate children's and young adults' books

1   Literary quality has nothing to do with apparent or real simplicity. The true simplicity of a children's story – the one that breaks through age boundaries – is often only achieved after extensive work.

2   As with any other story, in children's and young people's stories we must pay attention to the quality of the language, the solidity of the plot, etc., to which we must add the ability to captivate the reader. We are talking about readers who need to be enchanted and books that they will read out of interest and not on command. But that doesn't mean a writer is entitled to captivate his audience at all costs, just as, for example, an educator can't lie and present a made-up edifying story as real.

3   The most important thing about fiction is its content: sometimes the form is not perfect, but the story can nevertheless be valuable and so captivate the reader. It is not their job to give a complete view of a subject, and that means the reader needs to put some effort into getting the book's conclusions into the right perspective. It is the task of the educator to arm the young reader with a wider knowledge of the realities represented in the stories. Therefore, it is part of the educator's task to suggest relevant history books, biographies, reports, essays, other novels, etc.

4   Just as an historical story claim to be true, a fictional story should be plausible. Plausibility here is understood in the broad sense of what we find "convincing" according to the accumulated wisdom of humanity and, in many formal aspects, to what is common in our society. For example, some cartoons would not have been plausible centuries ago but could be now.

More information about the author via the QR code:
www.familyvalued.org/Luis-Daniel-Gonzalez-2

Anna Mendel

Author, Speaker and
Sensitivity Reader
Germany

Why do they stare like that, Mom?

Abstract

Many families cannot lead an undisturbed life, they experience discrimination based on various characteristics – both visible and invisible. Such families are exposed to individual and structural disadvantages and exclusion. Anna Mendel has Asian roots and three children, two of whom are disabled. She tells us about her family and how they are stared at in everyday life and in public. She explains how this affects her and how they deal with it as a family. Their stories can be a reminder to all those who are not aware of this kind of discrimination.

Article

Whenever the five of us step into the public eye, we are a play, a theatre, a show for others. We, that is my husband David and I, Anna, plus Simon, Lukas and Maya. Simon is autistic, Lukas has Down syndrome and Maya is just Maya. They are children of a so-called biracial (aka intercultural) marriage: my husband is white; I am a Southeast Asian woman of colour. For many, the high diversity of my family, which is also visible, seems to be a challenge.

When people see us, they have to dig deep into their artfully crafted and carefully sorted pigeonholes in order to categorize us correctly. That man and this woman: What's the story behind it? Does she speak our language? Did he bring her back from a vacation? Biracial marriages are now much more common, or much more obvious, than they were 10, 20 or 30 years ago. In other countries they have only been allowed since the last century – a leftover from colonialism.

Growing up in Stuttgart, people of colour were a part of our everyday lives. But for my husband it was completely new to be looked at as if we didn't belong. Back then, in the early 2010s, it was older couples in the department store elevator or in the park. Nowadays two exits on the highway towards the Swabian Alb hills make a difference. If we go to a hardware store that is a bit more rural we notice it immediately. "People stare. You'll have to get used to that when you're with me," I told my husband back when we became a couple. Many call it everyday racism, what we experience as a family. I feel it more as racism than as everyday life.

And then there is our Lukas with the visible disability, in public in a rehab buggy that is longer than it is wide and takes up a lot of space. At home he stays behind locked doors, high gates and always with an adult because, as soon as he feels that no one is watching, he runs away. But out here I need "the grip" – a strong grip around his wrist so that he doesn't run off or tear himself away. My pulse is racing. When we walk along the road, I sweat, and my awareness is increased. And then they look again, the people, they look and look away and look again.

Lukas stands out, of course, his eyes a little narrower due to his uncreased eyelids, his head smaller, his arms and legs shorter. Why is he screaming like that? Why is he lashing out? Why is he sitting in a pram at his age? Children are the most likely to ask these things, and parents and other adults do not have good answers for them. Many are afraid of an answer, so avoid asking. Others mean well and send the child over to us: "Just ask." No, no, don't just ask! We have enough to do ourselves, and my son is neither your child's social project nor an object of study for your own child rearing. Besides, he wouldn't be able to answer anyway; he is what we call nonverbal. He would answer "Ukas". He can do that, but for this achievement he needed 3 years of speech therapy. And after that you would get nothing more out of him. This is usually the point at which other children lose interest in him or start to make fun of him; because he makes noises or tries to tell a story with signs or gestures. They stop interacting with him, but they still stare.

And then there is Simon, not visibly disabled, but still conspicuous. Unusual noises and movements in public, no answers to "simple" questions, no understanding of social norms. He does not get on well with other children on the playground, and he speaks very differently from what many expect from an 8-year-old. Most adults say "you hardly notice it at all", but why doesn't he have any friends, and why does he go to a special school? And why is he so overwhelmed whenever it gets loud and stressful? On the other hand, he may just scream and cry for no obvious reason. And then the people stare again.

Being stared at is clearly challenge number 1 in our lives. Sometimes I don't even notice it anymore, but sometimes it's really very unpleasant. People forget their "good manners" and forget to continue eating or to keep on walking, because they're staring at us. For many years I have been trying to stay completely centred and prepare my children for what awaits them "outside". I give them all the self-confidence and knowledge that I didn't have at their age. I buy them books to explain their disabilities. I train myself in anti-racism. But in the end, I just have to find a child-friendly answer when they ask me: "*Why do they stare like that, Mom*?" You can find out more about Anna Mendel's work as an author, speaker and sensitivity reader here: annamendel.de. Her book "*WIR - Geschichten aus dem Alltag mit behinderten Kindern*", as well as her children's books "*Linus liebt Licht*" and "*Momo ist das alles viel zu viel*" about autistic children, are published by Brimboriumverlag. You can order them online from Brimboriumverlag.de.

Julia Kahle
CEO and Co-Founder
Germany

Balancing care and work: Make it as effective and easy as possible!

Abstract

Support for home care makes companies attractive. More years of work? More skilled workers? – More family-work compatibility! Companies must begin to deal with the care responsibilities of their employees in an appreciative and pragmatic way. To determine the true ROI of home-care benefits, it is essential for companies to include key indicators such as staff turnover, absenteeism, productivity levels, and employee satisfaction in their metrics.

Article

In an ageing society, millions of employees are faced with a double burden: care for loved ones and their own professions. This situation is a major challenge, not only for caregivers but also for employers. Studies from other countries show that the burden of employees' care obligations costs companies tens of billions of euros annually, mostly due to reduced productivity and absences.

In this country too, there is a lack of care structures that relieve the burden on family caregivers: Given the 98,000 daycare places nationwide, there are over four million people in need of care who live at home. That is a supply rate of just 2.3 percent.

Many employees are forced to reduce their working hours; but at the same time, the pressure on companies to retain sufficient skilled workers is increasing.

Making care support easily accessible

Companies have it in their own hands to give employees with care responsibilities the support they need. They can create their own structures and offerings to give employees relief and, at the same time, enable them to work more than the 33 hours per week that the average family caregiver works at their profession.

Flexible working hours, the possibility of working from home or special care leave days are known and established as measures. But is that enough? – It is always worthwhile to check whether employees are really using these measures. This is because support offerings from employers, though well-intentioned, often ignore the realities of employees' lives and are consequently hardly used.

New, low threshold offers can change that. More and more companies, for example, are relying on everyday support by nannies, which employees can book online as needed. This concept that has already proven itself in childcare is now being used in the care of elderly relatives as well.

Offering advice on home care

With the low-threshold access to home care an important step has been taken. But companies can do even more. Caring for relatives is usually accompanied by a high emotional burden and great uncertainty, especially while the situation is still unaccustomed. The employees affected have many questions – organizational, legal and financial. Here, too, companies can provide support by bundling in-house information and advisory services. Support and advice from a single source in a familiar environment save employees time-consuming research and help them quickly find their way into a new routine spanning home care and work.

An investment that pays off

The provision of innovative care benefits is not just a gesture of care – it is a wise investment. By supporting employees who have care responsibilities, companies can increase productivity and reduce absenteeism. In addition, the commitment to a better family-work balance contributes to an appreciative corporate culture and a positive employer branding. By showing that they take the needs of their employees seriously at all stages of life, companies remain attractive to existing and upcoming talent.

"Conclusion: Good for one, good for all"

With modern care benefits and appropriate advice companies give their employees relief in emotionally and organizationally challenging situations. They also unburden the teams and departments to which the affected colleagues belong. By ensuring that employees quickly acclimatize to the "new normal" of caring for relatives, they promote the productivity of individuals and the organization as a whole. At the same time, they give the workforce and potential applicants the assurance that they are still appreciated with all their diverse needs and challenges. In times of shortages of skilled workers, and given mandatory ESG reporting, this is an important signal that has a direct bearing on the "S" ("social") of that ESG report.

More information about the author via the QR code:
www.familyvalued.org/Julia-Kahle-2

Heiner Fischer

Founder Vaterwelten GmbH
Germany

The new role of fathers: challenges and opportunities

Abstract

The traditional role of the father has changed greatly in recent years. More and more men are striving for an active and equal role in the family, both in raising children and in partnerships. But this change brings both challenges and opportunities for men, women, families and society as a whole. The new role of fathers offers the opportunity to break down traditional role models and create a society based on equality, partnership and mutual support. Through the courage to change and the willingness to take on challenges, men, women and families can work together to shape a future that is characterized by respect, appreciation and equal opportunities.

Article

1)   **From desire to reality:** A father's personal development from the desire to take a more active role in the family to its realization, which entails challenges and self-reflection. The path leads from the assumption of responsibility to the search for a real family-work balance.

2)   **Societal change:** The increasing number of fathers who are actively involved in raising children reflects a societal change. However, this change also requires new ways of thinking in business and politics to empower men in their role as

fathers and give women the opportunity to pursue careers without having to forego caring for children.

3) **Challenges and opportunities:** Meeting the challenges that come with the new role of father also offers opportunities for personal growth, the strengthening family relationships and the creation of a more balanced society. Through self-reflection, exchange, and support, fathers can find new ways to shape their role while empowering their partners and children.

Conclusion:

Before I had children, I couldn't imagine how much soul-searching I would be doing later on. But already at the young age of 15 the desire to be a committed father had crystallized in me. My own father was not able to give me the fatherly support I needed. His professional obligations often left him absent; even at weekends his presence was missing when I needed it most. At the beginning of my third decade of life, this wish became reality when my partner and I became parents. From the very beginning, it was clear to me that I wanted to take an active role in the family, live my fatherhood responsibly and strive for an equal partnership. But my employer saw it differently and denied me parental leave beyond the two "fathers' months". When I expressed the desire to move to part-time work after parental leave, the employee/employer relationship broke down, and I decided to quit my secure job.

  This experience left a lasting impression on me. I put the family at the centre of my life and repeatedly encountered challenges as a man, a father and partner. On a personal level, I didn't just learn during the moments when I carried my children around, put them to bed, read to them or changed their diapers. I also rethought my childhood and my relationship with my own father. Between ideals and reality there often lies one's own upbringing, and many things that I would have liked to do differently turned out to be challenging to implement. I founded a fathers' group at the Krefeld Child Protection Association and found allies there. Every 14 days we exchange ideas about our role as fathers and grow from the shared experiences we have with our children, our partners and our employers. We encounter obstacles to our taking on an active father role and look for solutions together, find solace in our discussions.

More and more fathers are taking an active role in the family and striving to play an equal role in raising children. These are positive developments in our society. However, the Corona pandemic made it clear that, in times of crisis, child rearing is increasingly being taken over by women again. A similar phenomenon is currently evident in daycare centres, where we are facing a daycare crisis. By 2035, there will be a deficit of up to 7 million workers, including carers in daycare centres. The childcare situation is deteriorating year on year, and parents have to think about who can take over. Meanwhile companies are urgently looking for skilled workers. New measures are needed to strengthen families on the one hand, and to secure economic strength in Germany on the other.

With Vaterwelten ("Fathers' Worlds") we have developed an approach that strengthens men in their role as fathers and gives women the opportunity to pursue a career. It is no longer enough to simply bring women back into the company after giving birth. For real family-work balance, and an increased employment rate, we must strengthen the role of men in the family. For over four years digital discussion forums have been taking place at vaterwelten.de, in which we talk about fatherhood, partnership, family-work compatibility and everyday family life. At lectures I am often introduced as an expert on fathers, and at the same time have to point out that I, too, am only human and merely the sum of my experiences. I tell you about my doubts as a father, the painful rejections of my children, which cut like razor blades. I practice self-reflection, have numerous conversations and am patient; I talk a lot about it with my partner. I am very grateful to her for making it possible for me to be a father and for seeing me as an equal partner in the family - this is a key success factor for my fatherhood.

"Change must take place on three levels: individual, structural, and political"

On an individual level, fathers have to learn new skills and change. This can be done through self-study or conversation with other men. In particular, it is crucial that men spend time alone with their children to develop new skills. The role of women is important here too, as they need to give fathers the space to actively fulfil their role.

Their competence advantage must keep pace with that of fathers. At the structural level, companies and institutions need to support fathers. More than 1.7 million fathers are currently considering quitting their jobs to improve their family–career balance. It is therefore important that companies forge an emotional bond with fathers, and that family support institutions and daycare centres adapt to the new fathers. They should consciously involve fathers in the care obligations instead of automatically calling the mother.

After all, these changes can only succeed if the political framework is conducive. Although Germany has been offering parental leave and parental allowance since 2007, the latter has not been adjusted for inflation since then. Many families cannot afford to take parental leave, and fathers have to continue working to secure the family income. The implementation of the "family startup time", an EU regulation that should have been in implementation since 2019, could offer a solution here. Parents would receive 14 days of leave with full pay to take care of the newborn and the family.

More information about the author via the QR code:
www.familyvalued.org/Heiner-Fischer-2

Sibylle Patriarca

Social pedagogue and family counsellor
Germany

"The place on my right... remains empty" – when a relative dies and leaves a gap

Abstract

Death, grief and loss are part of our humanity. But what if it is your own child, or a parent is suddenly no longer there? What effects does this have on the family system? How do we deal with grief, and how do we maintain trust and confidence in life? My contribution is an invitation for families to deal more consciously with this often invisible and always undesired situation in everyday life.

Article

Already at the time of birth, the only certain thing in life is that we will die! We humans are often reluctant to face this fact; we exclude it and suppress it until, at some point, a death occurs in our close family circle. Dying and death, grief and pain, loss and farewell are essential parts of our humanity. But what if it is your own (possibly yet unborn) child or mom/dad who are sudcenly no longer there?

Very often it is especially with our parents that we have the longest relationship of our lives; with our mothers it is as if the umbilical cord is cut for a second time. Through the death of a parent a piece of childhood is buried, and the children move to new places, that is, they have to grow into new roles in the family "system". Let us forget the idea that everything is fine again after the "first year of mourning".

Grief for a child or a parent will accompany relatives for the rest of their lives. Let us also understand that the lives of the bereaved are changing, and that they will also change themselves through what they have experienced.

Five phases of grief over a loss

(according to Elisabeth Kübler-Ross, 1986-2004, psychiatrist and death researcher)
How long or how intensively these phases last depends on how old the person is, on what previous experiences they have already had with regard to bereavement, on the way in which the loss occurred, on their resilience, and on whether there exists a network of supportive people.

Phase 1: Denial

The reality of loss is not accepted. Sufferers often deny that the loss has really happened or try to distort reality to alleviate the pain. Needs in grief change very quickly in this phase: one minute the bereaved has a desire for a visit or a conversation, and then suddenly they would rather be alone. For adults it is important to be as gentle, authentic and honest as possible with children; they cope best with that. Say when you're overwhelmed, when don't know what to say or do, or have no idea how go about things. Have a conversation with your child about his or her view of life, death and grief. Depending on how old the child is, his access to the spiritual world is natural and not a matter of fear. Explain to children the importance of the grave, the cemetery and the funeral. Joint rituals strengthen and stabilize the child internally. Always refer to the deceased by name when they are spoken of, not obliquely or in the form of an event or stroke of fate.

Phase 2: Anger

After denial, anger often occurs. Those affected are angry with themselves, with others, with the loss itself or even with higher powers. This anger can be directed against everything that is related to the loss. It is important not to deny grieving people this anger and the thoughts that come with it. It is advisable not to take their words and behaviours personally or to react with similar anger and defensiveness.

Phase 3: Negotiation

In this phase people often try to negotiate with their pain. They try to negotiate with God and the universe to somehow reverse or undo the loss. This can come in the form of promises, prayers, or negotiations. The death of a loved one inevitably confronts us with the fear of our own death. This confrontation can trigger deep-seated fears or a guilty conscience.

Phase 4: Depression

The fourth phase often involves a deep sadness or depression about the loss. Those affected withdraw, feel hopeless or empty and have difficulty feeling joy. It is appropriate to let people grieve in their own individual way.

"When you are sad, look back into your heart, and you will see that you are really crying for what was your joy." (Kahlil Gibran)

This quote emphasizes the inseparable connection between joy and sadness. Often, we see both emotions as opposites, but in reality they are mutually dependent. Without sadness we cannot feel true joy, without joy we cannot understand what it is like to be sad. Joy and sadness help us appreciate the ups and downs of life. Without sadness, joy would not be so deep and meaningful, without joy we would not be able to overcome sadness. Overall, it is important to accept, integrate, and experience both joy and sadness, as they both play important emotional and existential roles in our lives. They are two sides of the same coin and allow us to understand and appreciate life in all its facets. Touch and physical contact can bring healing. If you are unsure whether you should hug or gently lay your hands on the bereaved, just ask them.

Phase 5: Acceptance

People begin to accept the loss and adapt to a world in which the deceased family member no longer exists. This does not necessarily mean that the pain has disappeared, but rather that the human being has found ways, possibilities and strategies

within himself that enable him to live with the loss, to integrate the pain into life, to look forward and to build something new.

The two most powerful means against forgetting are remembering and listening. What is our favourite memento of the deceased person? What connects us internally with them, beyond time and space? It is both sensible and important to talk about the deceased family member again and again, to tell each other about our experiences, to share stories and to listen empathetically without making value judgments.

"*The Last Word*" comes from a conversation with a mother and father who had lost their child: "*What did your son leave you?*" "Us, he left us there... and our love, our love has become even stronger. He left us the task of caring for it, letting it flourish and growing from it!" So "*the place on my right will remain empty*", yet full of memories, value and purpose!

More information about the author via the QR code:
www.familyvalued.org/Sibylle-Patriarca-2

Rosa Pich

Author

Spain

How to be happy with 1, 2, 3... children?

Abstract

The title of this article is also the title of a book I wrote a few years ago. It was born out of a desire to share with others my experience as the mother of a large family. For years I have been asked: How do you manage everything, Rosa? So, I decided to write down my experience and my methods, so that many families can benefit from it. Do not expect any revolutionary methods here. We just describe our family life, how we organize it, how we surmount our daily challenges. The loss of three children has brought us closer together and matured us. Faith was the supporting power. When people ask me my secret, I answer quite simply: My deep faith in God.

Article

In this article, I would like to outline in a few pages how we organize life together in our family. It is a large family in the 21st century, living in a large city in Catalonia, Spain. Both my husband and I come from large families, so we already had experience. The basis for this article is a book, with the same title, that I wrote a few years ago.

Eating together

The midday meal is the most important meeting of the day. It is an opportunity for everyone in the family to share their experiences and personal anecdotes in a warm and friendly atmosphere. In large families, daily meals are usually simple, because parents who work outside the home don't have much time to cook. More important than the food are the conversations at the table. It is important that parents bring a current topic to the table, to educate children and to give them criteria for evaluation. It is also to learn what the children think, to teach them whether something is right or wrong, and ultimately to find solutions to problems.

In our family we laugh a lot at these meetings, because everyone can tell funny anecdotes. At table we live by the motto, "*Serve your neighbour*". Look to see whether they want more water, if they want bread, they don't have a napkin, want a second helping etc. By the way, children have to learn to eat everything that comes on the table, and we try to get them to take a little of what they don't like.

Teamwork in the family

In our house we all form a team and help each other. We know each other very well, including our weaknesses and strengths. Everyone in the family has an annual development plan. This hangs on the kitchen wall. Mom needs to improve on the following point, for example: "*Don't boss dad around.*" My husband tells me I already have enough children to give orders to, so I can just give him a break. At the beginning of the school year, the whole family meets, and we assign the household chores together: setting the table, clearing the table, etc. The children do the assignments in pairs: an older one takes care of a little one. In this way, they learn from an early age to feel that the household is their own. Making a bed, for example, is possible from the age of two if taught properly.

School-Kids-Parents

And now we tackle the subject of school. We try to meet with the teachers of each child once a quarter. The first thing we talk about is not the grades, but the behaviour of our children, both in class and with their classmates. We expect our children to take care of all their classmates. In our family, our children know that their greatest responsibility is to learn, and that we expect from each one according to their abilities. As parents we have a responsibility to know what the abilities of each child really are, not just what we would like them to be.

Child raising

Over the years we have gained a lot of experience in raising children, which we would like to give back here in a condensed form. As we said above, the older ones are mentors for the younger ones. But the ultimate responsibility for raising the children lies with the parents. However, not everyone knows how to educate. Parents usually need time to learn parenting methods and thus become better parents and friends of their children. It seems to me that we always have to be ready to say NO to our children, even when they cry.

Children constantly put us to the test and expect us to set limits for them. They want us to stay with "no" when dad says "no" anc not change our minds just because the child goes crying to mom. Sometimes tired mothers give sweets to children to keep them quiet. In doing so, they are doing them a disservice. Children need to hear a firm and final "no". We must not change our minds just because the child throws a tantrum. A good recipe for every marriage and every family is humour: to be able to laugh at mistakes and quirks. Likewise, we must be humble: ready to ask and receive forgiveness whenever necessary.

"Value people for what they are, not for what they have"

I also have some advice on the subject of money: We need to keep the children very short of money. Parents apparently give their children too much money. In doing so, they are doing children a disservice. Modern electronics can facilitate communication with the children, but they carry serious risks: inactive children who spend the day in front of the TV, or playing video games, are often flabby and irritable. Children need us to set limits for them. There are three categories: some things are allowed

for everyone, others only above a certain age; and finally, the third category, forbidden for everyone, such as smoking at home.

Any punishments we give to our children must be proportionate and well-considered. It is precisely here that a harmonious interlocking of love and educational effect can be seen. In some families, there are hardly any guardrails. It is those children who are allowed to do anything who are unfortunate. And, talking about punishment, praise must not be absent. At home we congratulate children when they have done a good job - but only then. Undeserved praise - as given in some families - confuses the children and is harmful to their upbringing. Children often behave differently from what we would like. This can lead to stressful situations, and some mothers tend to become hysterical in such cases. My advice is, toughen up and don't make a big deal out of it. Of course, not everyone can manage that. But we should at least try.

Marital relationship

The marital relationship forms the foundation of the family. Here are a few words about it. I don't understand some friends who tell me in conversation: "*I love my husband very much, but the ones I really love are my children*". Communication in marriage is fundamental. This is confirmed by all marriage counsellors and psychologists. That's why we sometimes leave the house so that we can talk to each other undisturbed. Sometimes simple topics are on the agenda, other times opinions are far apart. Peace and time are what is required here. A golden rule here is never to argue in front of the children. The children are aware that we have different priorities and preferences, but arguing in front of the children is a no-go.

Conjugal life is also part of the marital relationship. You can't be a hard worker, a great father to your children, and not care about your conjugal life. And we must not neglect the sexual aspect of marriage. Many marital problems would be solved if we were more willing and proactive in bed.

One doesn't just marry a man or a woman but an entire family: parents-in-law, brothers-in-law and sisters-in-law. I am careful not to directly rebuke or comment on their behaviour. If a comment is necessary, then my husband will do it, not me. And last but not least, the topic of taking care of your appearance. My father always told me: "*Rosa, you have to take care of yourself*". I used to downplay this because I considered it rather hedonistic. Later I understood that he was right.

Seeing children as a gift

In the 21st century, many people consider children a burden. In ancient times, now and always, children are an incomparable gift. But sadly, some do not see it that way. They see children as a kind of slavery, and a very expensive one at that.

"In the 21st century, many people think that children are a burden"

But the opposite is the case. Children help us to be happy, to come out of ourselves and to give ourselves to others with joy. Friends ask me, how many children should we have? My advice: "*The more you love, the happier you are*". Each married couple must determine the number for themselves. I won't give any advice on that. Human laws are made by people, and they are not binding if they violate human nature and common sense. Everyone in the world knows that killing your own child is the very worst thing you can do. As I understand it, we pass on life because we are open to it. I grew up with this mindset and that's how we think in our family today.

My secret

We are coming to the end. I am always asked how I find time for work and so much more in addition to a household with so many children. My answer is very simple: God. To see God as Father, as a friend. My relationship with God is the source from which I draw my strength, my inspiration, and my peace. I would be happy if my children also developed a direct relationship with God, but our principle is freedom. In our home, prayer is not obligatory because we respect the freedom of our children. But we do explain to them that it helps us to be better people, more human.

Conclusion: My secret is my relationship with God.

More information about the author via the QR code:
www.familyvalued.org/Rosa-Pich-2

Prof.
Michael Schulte-Markwort
Child and adolescent psychiatrist
Germany

Family years – how our life with children succeeds

Abstract

In this article, we want to look at some aspects of family life: foundation, structure, dangers and limits. My book of the same title serves as the basis for this article. Below are a few sentences for orientation about the content of the article. Family is the primordial cell of society. Primary love enables bonding within the family. Food is an important part of family life, and the dining table is a meeting place for the family. Raising children must be defined by trust. Excessive anxiety on the part of parents paralyses the development of children and limits their autonomy. A balanced approach to praising the child is necessary in order to give the child correct feedback. Praising has to be learned, the same applies to saying no and to the "so-called" punishments.

What makes a family?

Family is a wonderful expression of connectedness. This includes the emotional bond between the family members, i.e. within the so-called primary love. This is distinguished from secondary love, which refers rather to infatuation ("being in love") and friendship. Part of what defines family is its relevance for society. This relevance results from the fact that the family is the primordial cell of society. It ensures

181

society's survival. In other words, the family is the primordial cell for our living to-gether in society.

Family circle

Family life is very varied. Today I would like to emphasize the aspect of "everyone at the same table". That phrase fits very well with this one: "*Food is an expression of love*". The way a family eats together reflects directly its mental health and connect-edness. The food establishes a connection with the person who prepared it, usually a parent. What is cooked, what is prepared, thus connects children with their parents. The sentence: "*It tastes best at mom's*" shows the emotional bond that food creates. Such sentences are heard not only from the children, but also from the husbands. The dining table plays a decisive role in families because of the aforementioned bond. The table is at the same time a meeting place, buffet, marketplace, comfort blanket, conference venue and playground for the family. The family identity is an important part of the whole: common values and a common language. From a psychological point of view, every person needs their own identity; and the same applies to the family.

Importance of motherhood

It should be our concern to give motherhood the status it deserves in society as a whole. During pregnancy, an intimate and intense relationship develops between mother and child, which continues after birth until the end of life. A better acknowl-edgement of motherhood could, among other things, lead to new pension models and prospective entitlements. At present it is still the income generated by working mothers that is prized, rather than the fact that they raise our children. My message to mothers: "*Enjoy your motherhood and don't "hide it under a bushel". Be proud of yourself and of your child. In doing so, you make the world a little more valuable and lay the foundation for something great: a happy child in a wonderful family.*" Nowa-days, every self-determined mother can and must decide whether she wants to work and pursue a career. Mother and father should then have absolutely equal rights. Child-rearing must not be an expression of oppression and incapacitation, and we should all appreciate more the extraordinary achievements of mothers. Mothers must never be forced into housework by others, under any circumstances.

Parenting

In my book "Family Years" I aim to encourage parents to "trust in yourself and in your child". Primary love actually leads to a trusting relationship between parent and child. But as the child gets older and more independent, some parents lose this trust. This is partly due to the fact that our pedagogy is deficit oriented. The solution would be to give the children more confidence here. Now let us move on to the topic of "overparenting" and the anxiety of some parents. If the parents are overly anxious then they try to isolate the children – a phenomenon we call "overparenting". The consequence of this is that the children become immature. The decisive factor here is a balanced parental attitude to the topic of risk assessment. And now we switch to the topic of punishment. In my opinion, children need feedback when something goes wrong, but no harshness, no punishments, hardly any disciplinary measures. What they need most is that we set them an example of appropriate behaviour.

I am often shocked with how much mistrust children are treated. But it is this mistrust that elicits insincerity from the child, and not the other way around. Dealing with children "on equal terms" does not mean burdening the child with adult problems. Due respect for the child always takes into account the child's capabilities.

Children without prohibitions move more freely and confidently. This is what my experience in the practice has taught me. What I mean by that is not to make a big issue out of the "no". Of course, there must be a "no" here and there when people live together. Nor do you always have to explain the reason for setting limits for children. It's enough to say: "*That's the way it is for now, because I say so!*" How much autonomy do children need? The parents' trust in the child provides the basis for the child's autonomy. The degree of autonomy allowed depends on the personality of the child; some want a lot, others less. Moreover, personality disorders of the parents can also have a negative impact on the child's autonomy. Another aspect of raising children is helping them to find their sexual identity. The conviction that you can change boys' and girls' natures simply through the choice of their toys is not true.

Role of parents

Secure – that is, emotionally stable – parents do not need to compete with each other and can complement each other constructively. If a child is born and the insecure father feels like a loser, then this is not a good starting point for constructive cooperation. Let's now come to the important topic of praise. Praise must not be given for just any action, otherwise it becomes emotionally devalued. Parents need to decide on the basis of the child's self-confidence when the praise is appropriate, and what kind of praise. Children must be able to rely on their parents to love them. However, this does not mean that parents must approve of everything their children do. The points above are a quick discourse on some aspects of family life. I hope readers were nevertheless able to find helpful hints for themselves.

More information about the author via the QR code:
www.familyvalued.org/Michael-Schulte-Markwort-2

Felicitas Richter

Speaker, Author & Mentor
Germany

"Have you started living yet or are you still optimizing?" Mastering the interplay of family and career with ease

Abstract

Sometimes parents experience everyday life as a hurricane – they don't know whether they're on their head or their heels, so they try to compensate by planning everything to the last detail. That is precisely the right moment to go where it is quietest: to your own centre. There you can recharge your batteries and clear your head, and THEN you can start planning everyday life. That way you'll find more joy, ease and serenity in the successful interplay of family and career.

Article

My daughter once put it in a nutshell. One stressful Easter Saturday, she said: "*Mom, the most important thing for us children is not having the most beautiful celebration with Easter eggs and presents, or even that you are always there for us. The most important thing is that you take good care of yourself and are relaxed.*" Her words reminded me again of something very important: Our everyday life as parents is their childhood and youth. But how do we shape an everyday life in which there is room for everything– children, partnership, dependent relatives, voluntary work, professional work and even ourselves? How do we stay centred in these turbulent times?

There is a saying, "*Work doesn't go away when you show your child the rainbow. But the rainbow won't wait until you've finished the work either.*" Children live for the moment, and they show us the excitement of the moment. However, when our heads are too full, we often notice the rainbow only fleetingly. If we nevertheless allow ourselves to be amazed along with the child, we discover many things that bring us joy, strength and calm. We find our centre when we consciously experience what we do – take a shower without thinking about the to-do list; taste how delicious the strawberry from the garden is, heedless of the housework; immerse ourselves in a picture book without thinking about the emails that we still have to answer.

Drawing strength from what surrounds us is one thing, planning regular moments of leisure is another: moments in which we do what is good for us. A daily walk after dinner, a fixed free evening for each parent, and a weekly night out for the couple often work wonders and recharge our batteries. Single parents too need help if they are to have any regular free time. Many parents suffer from the way that the "hurricane" runs their lives, and they want more creative freedom so that they can simply "start living". This can be achieved if we sometimes break the mould: instead of serving everyone at the family celebration, sit down and join the conversation. Instead of always being the one to raise your hand at the Parent-Teacher-Association meeting, endure the silence when no one else volunteers.

You don't have to win the battle alone. In order to accomplish everything that is important to family in everyday life, team spirit is needed. Parents should not only share tasks in their partnership, but also responsibilities. Weekly family meetings can help children understand how to get involved. Support and offer relief to family, friends and other networks. Parents are allowed both to accept and to ask for help – trusting that other people will be happy to help. Furthermore, external and paid support can provide valuable rest and recuperation in turbulent times - be it through a home-help or a delivery service.

I firmly believe:

Children don't need an optimized childhood; they need a spirited one.

Children don't need a pampering; they need encouragement and trust.

Children don't need perfect parents; they need happy parents.

More information about the author via the QR code:

http://www.familyvalued.org/Felicitas-Richter-2

Carolina and Carlos Aponte

School director and Entrepreneur
Colombia

The everyday life of a large family

Abstract

Starting a large family is a decision that the newlywed couple makes together. A large family means more work, but also more joy. It gives life a deeper meaning. It is a legacy for posterity. Watching children grow and develop fills parents with a deep and inner joy. The professional career has to take a back seat, but the joy of having children does not stand up to comparison. Our children are brought up in a value-oriented way. They will later ensure a stable, peaceful and more just society.

Interview

#1: How did the idea of starting a large family come about?

We met at the age of 18 and 20, in the middle of a turbulent time in Colombia, 3 presidential candidates had just been murdered, the drug trade showed its military power, and the constitutional reform of 1991 had been agreed upon after more than 150 years of the country's history. But we shared the same attitude to life from the beginning: "*The true transformative power of society lies in the love that emanates from a family.*"

Carolina came from a well-structured family that her parents were able to sustain by breaking their own family's previous harmful cycle. Carlos, on the other hand, came from a dysfunctional family in which the father figure left much to be desired due to

various tragedies in 4 previous generations. We knew that thanks to the revival of our faith at World Youth Day in Paris in 1997, God would be on our side. At that time, however, we were thinking of a family with 4 children: not only child, but we also said, nor two, because they would compare; neither do three, because there is always one left in the sandwich. But from there to 9 was a long way. Well, the 9 are the consequence of a yes that we said to ourselves at that time: *To be open to life*! Open to give us the opportunity to love one another, to live in the truth and to welcome each child: a new child was always going to be welcome!

#2: What does it mean for parents to have more children than usual?
We married at the age of 23 and 25. That is, directly after our study periods. We wanted to start an extended family. Our friends told us: a) we would ruin our lives, b) we should rather "enjoy" life or c) we would not have access to good jobs. Everyone thinks and speaks according to their own worldview. We ignored the comments mentioned above. The well-intentioned advice even came from people close by. With our plans - they said - we would just make life difficult for ourselves. Practically everyone does that, right? Everyone sacrifices themselves for what is important.

In the month of August 2024, we will celebrate 25 years of marriage. For the first 17 years, Carlos was the one who made the money. In the beginning, he worked in Colombia in the telecommunication sector and later took on various jobs abroad. This brought him to Canada while Carolina, wanted to rise our children by herself, ran the household in Colombia and then Canada. When we already had 7 children, Carlos got job offer in the USA and another to go back to Colombia. All these works American- corporate aspirations kind of style could distract us from our family goals. It was the moment to examine the priorities and rearrange them. The good thing about it was that in a large family it is more difficult to break away from family obligations. It's a constant reality check that helps you mature organically over the years. Carlos accepted then that job offers in Colombia. It was a job at the university, i.e. something different from the IT sector (The telecommunication sector was evolving into the IT sector). This change was sorely needed, among other things, because Carolina fell ill during that time. In addition, the older daughters reached puberty age. For their training, we needed a suitable environment where our values were lived. In addition, the two youngest were born just right after that time we came back.

To make it even more exciting, Carlos got sick during that time. Thank God Carolina was healthy again in the meantime. She was able to take up a new job near where we live. This new beginning promoted her personal development. And this development has had a positive effect on the children. Since then, Carlos has borne the brunt of the burden at home. He now has a predominantly remote job, so that the compatibility of family and career works for him. What really matters is, if the #1 entrepreneurship of our lives, one of the parents has to "*keep an eye on the ball*" in order to not get lost

#3: Can you confirm that children from large families have a deeper sense of responsibility?

We would agree, as long as parents don't make their children feel like a burden. *"I regret many things in my life, but never my children!"* We usually tell them: You are the best thing that could have happened to any of us. Unfortunately, we are aware of cases in which older children in particular take on tasks that are not age appropriate. Children must be treated like potential adults. And there are also cases in which the underage children are neglected in large families.

We are organized in such a way that children are given tasks for which they are responsible. This creates a team spirit. As a result, children grow up with more autonomy. This is necessary because parents cannot do everything. And because children learn to enjoy the successes in their tasks. Being the parent of a large family has undoubtedly shaped our character. It has opened our eyes to the beauty of life. This was only possible because we granted the children this autonomy. In contrast, there are parents who want to keep everything under control. They think they are more prudent than others. We call them helicopter parents.

#4: More children mean more work at home. How can family responsibilities be reconciled with a job in a company outside the home?

We have organized our household in such a way that the children receive age-appropriate assignments. This allows you to cope with the tasks without hectic and stress. As mentioned above, this approach promotes their autonomy, their independence and their mutual support: older people help the younger ones. In our family, we avoid raising selfish children. Anything else leads to great bitterness in life, for the child and for the family.

"True happiness for us parents is the children who love the truth and are kind to one another."

With our concept, the children learn to work and be useful in the family. In the time when this was not enough, we have employed maids for the household. For this purpose, we parents have chosen jobs that enable a strong participation at home. It must not happen that our children remember, after our death, that we have neglected them only because we have been intensively involved in the work. Then it would be said that they lacked affection and tenderness because of it.

#5: In some large families, older children contribute financially to family costs. What do you think of that?

Well, in our case, they are already starting to earn money for their own expenses so that they can realize their own dreams. We wanted to be gentle on this matter, respecting the freedom of children, but at the same time inviting them to use the gift of life that has been given to them to proactively shape their own lives. We have seen cases in which parents die, and children take over the education of their siblings of their own volition, and in almost all cases it is as if life has rewarded them for this gesture of generosity.

#6: Do the older ones take care of the little ones in the family?

We are aware that the responsibility ultimately lies with us parents, but we encourage the children to support each other. Above all, we want older children to set a good example. Here is a concrete example. A few years ago, I received a scholarship from the Israeli government. This made it possible for us to travel to the Holy Land. However, the prerequisite for this was that the three adult daughters take care of the little ones. Otherwise, it wouldn't have worked. It was a blessing and a life experience for all of us.

#7: What are your three most important topics?
Respect for each other, a sense of reality and generosity, raising children in freedom.

#8: What recommendation would you give to a young couple who want to have three or more children?
That it is a blessing for parents and children alike, a large family. It means sacrifice, as with everything that is really worthwhile in life. A family is created step by step, day by day. It is important to maintain family time with good sense of humor. And to create spaces for dialogue between the coup e and to consistently protect these times. The priorities in the family must be set correctly: God first, then the couple, the children, the grandparents, the siblings. And only then does professional life come. From our point of view, this is the correct order. And it has proven itself with us: You find a work for a living not living to work. Living for other make the ego get in control

Many problems in families have their origin in the wrong order. But also, because the couple relationship has lost strength after a few years of marriage. Children should be educated to be independent so that they gradually learn to make good decisions. And another tip: The professional career is a means to an end, not the goal.

More information about the authors via the QR code:
www.familyvalued.org/Carolina-Carlos-Aponte-2

Janina Kürschner

Development worker in family and career

Mathias Kürschner

Author, Speaker, Appointment Navigator

Germany

Celebrating in a Meaningful Way – On the Cultural-Forming Power of Community in Family and Society

Abstract

Values are produced by formative community. A crucial occasion on which communities reassure themselves of their values is the festivals they celebrate. We have developed a festival concept in our family to encourage the family. We see the family as a powerhouse for conveying value. This has a considerable influence on the friendly environment, such as the neighbourhood and urban society.

Article

It is said that the Germans – unlike the French or Italians, for example – do not know how to celebrate. At best, the witty Rhinelander is granted a certain special competence here. However, we are not sure whether celebration is primarily a question of temperament or rather a question of mindfulness. **Because celebration means, first of all, the ability to organize interruptions in everyday life in order to reassure ourselves of the values that are important to us**. Holidays are deliberately set rhythms of change, where we make sure of certain values that are usually

related to this day. In the unwieldy slang of the 19th century, our Basic Law speaks here of days of "spiritual elevation", on which we break through the mill of the synchronized monotony of weekdays and, for example, on Sunday with a view to our Creator, make sure in a divine service that we were not created for the sake of work, but are interesting and valuable for our own sake. The Basic Law murmurs in a baroque way: "Human dignity is inviolable." Our solitary holidays, whether they are politically or religiously filled, also tell of the pointed stops of the annual calendar, so that we can leave the hamster wheel for a short time and reassure ourselves of our religious, historical or cultural identity.

Figure: At the Reformation Festival, Janina and Mathias Kürschner transform into Käthe and Martin Luther for their guests.

Now, however, it is up to the commitment of the individual to celebrate these festivals accordingly, to give them the correspondingly "memorable" framework, so that they are then also remembered accordingly! **As a family, for example, we felt the motivation to give the Reformation Festival a little more glamour than Halloween, which took place at the same time, because we simply knew that we belonged to the emancipatory achievements of the Reformation more than horror and horror.** But how do you celebrate that? How do you give it an appealing framework?

We started with a medieval costume party, to which we invited neighbours and friends in a private setting. My husband became Martin Luther, and I slipped into the role of his wife Käthe. We designed the greeting of the guests as a festive table speech and delighted the younger among them with the tactile enjoyment of eating chicken by hand. In between, there were short Luther impulses, which contained alternating pithy sayings of the eloquent reformer or smaller pieces on Christian freedom, the importance of conscience, or the value of the Christian faith against fear.

"Celebrate the festivals as they fall!"

At the festive table, the **everyday interrupting effect of the festival** can soon be felt. The conversations at the table then revolve around the benefits and disadvantages of religiosity for life. People think about their faith biographies (and their breakdowns). People ponder the value of bourgeois defensive rights against the state, individuality, freedom of the press and freedom of opinion. While strange figures crow "trick or treat" outside on the street, we made ourselves comfortable with the spirits we called ourselves... In the meantime, we celebrate the Reformation Festival with suckling pig and historicizing music in a community context, invite interview guests and keep shedding light on new achievements of the Reformation. What was previously more or less a blank space in the church's calendar of celebrations is now enthusiastically celebrated by many as a lesson in Protestant faith identity.

This does not always succeed. **If you want to celebrate, you have to be able to fail.** With our still small children, we wanted to integrate a "Sunday welcome party" into the weekly schedule. At that time, we lived in post-socialist Potsdam,

where Sunday was a kind of vacuum cleaner day for most citizens. Of course, something like this is also an interruption of the dusty monotony of everyday life. But we thought there was more to it: We wanted to point to God's work of creation and, just like the Jews ring in the Shabbat, prepare for Sunday accordingly. Mom has ceremoniously set the table for this. A few songs were sung with guitar accompaniment and prayers were said. The children found it "so semi" and dad was already thinking slightly impatiently about the beloved sports show on Saturday evening. The focus on Sunday lacked a little inner conviction and the ritual-artistic implementation was probably too unwieldy.

Both worked much better at a third celebration: We set up a neighbourhood meeting in an old villa district, which we introduced as just such a "salon" in allusion to the literary and political salons of the 19th century in Paris and Berlin. We invited quite high-class speakers, whom we interviewed about their professional background and also asked about their foundation of values. In the course of the evening, the guests from the neighbourhood were also included in the conversation with their questions and comments. And long after the end of the official part, people stood with wine and finger food spread all over the apartment and literally talked about God and the world, after the speaker discussion had set an appropriate setting beforehand. **People were happy to finally be able to skip the tormenting "what-do-you-do-where-from-from" platitudes and to be able to exchange ideas with others about burning life topics without much ado.**

Why did it work so well? Because it was culturally well embedded in the customs of the mostly aristocratic social elites there, with their lecture culture and their champagne receptions. And yet the salons were a thematic interruption of an everyday life that usually revolves around very superficially functional things such as comfort and the preservation or increase of vested rights. People reacted to this with great gratitude and affection, especially since we demonstrated and sought closeness in a rather distant, status-conscious milieu with the opening of our own four walls and a corresponding communication approach. Even years after we moved away from Potsdam, we meet people who cannot emphasize enough how much they miss celebrating the salons and to what extent "our" district had a positive influence on them in those years.

These and other examples are an encouragement to us that, despite some deplorable social developments, **there can be so much transforming and trend-setting power in the cultural contribution of small intact communities** that we would like to call on families in particular: *Celebrate the festivals as they fall!* Celebrate them creatively and full of lust, so that people pause and realize what values are worth living for in the 21st century.

More information about the authors via the QR code:

http://www.familyvalued.org/Janina-Mathias-Kuerschner-2

Doreen Amlung
Life compass Coach
Germany

Strong women – strong families

Abstract

In a hectic world, women's strength is the foundation of a healthy family. Discover how you can increase your inner strength and let it shine through simple changes in everyday life. Be inspired to find your balance and positively influence your environment – laughter included!

Artikel

The power of women

A woman who stands in her power is a gift not only for herself, but also for her loved ones. She has the ability to feed her family, not only with food, but also with love, wisdom and care. This strength is not always innate but can be developed and nurtured. Here are three simple tips on how you can increase your inner strength in everyday life and thus enrich your family.

#Tipp 1: Make self-care a priority

Self-care is not a luxury, but a necessity. You can only give what you have yourself. If your energy levels are low, you'll quickly get burned out and stressed. So treat yourself to little breaks regularly. A relaxing bath, a short meditation or a walk with

your dog – these little moments will help you recharge your batteries. Learn to say "no" and set clear limits. You're a superhero – but superheroes also need to refuel regularly.

#Tipp 2: Positive Affirmations and Self-Talk

The way you talk to yourself has a huge impact on your well-being. Negative self-talk pulls you down and weakens your inner power. Start the day with positive affirmations. Stand in front of the mirror and tell yourself things like: "I am strong", "I am sufficient", "I am loved". These simple phrases can work wonders and boost your confidence. It may seem a bit strange at first, but give it a try – you'll feel the difference.

#Tipp 3: Drink lemon water in the morning

A simple but effective nutrition tip is to drink a glass of warm lemon water every morning. This little habit has numerous benefits for your health:

1) Boosts the immune system: Lemons are rich in vitamin C, which supports your immune system and makes you more resistant to colds and other illnesses.

2) Promotes digestion: Lemon water stimulates the production of digestive juices and helps to get the stomach going. It can also help reduce unpleasant bloating.

3) Detoxifies the body: Lemon water supports the liver in its detoxification work and helps to flush harmful substances out of the body.

4) Hydrates the body: After a night of sleeping, your body is often dehydrated. A glass of lemon water will give you a hydrating start to the day.

5) Improves skin: The antioxidant properties of vitamin C and other nutrients in lemons help cleanse the skin and give it a fresh, healthy glow.

To make lemon water, simply squeeze the juice of half a lemon into a glass of warm water. Drink it immediately after getting up on an empty stomach. This little morning routine can make a big difference in your overall well-being.

Laughter is the best medicine

And never forget: Humor is a wonderful source of strength. Laughter reduces stress, strengthens the immune system and connects us with others. So find reasons to laugh – whether it's through a funny movie, a funny book, or just fooling around with your family. Laughter is contagious and will lift the mood in your home.

Final Thoughts

Strong women build strong families. When you stand in your power, you are a shining example for your children and partner. You show them that it is possible to go through life with love, strength and wisdom. And that's exactly what we need in this world: women who know how valuable they are and who share this power with their family and the world. Stay in your power, radiate your light and see how your environment changes for the better.

More information about the author via the QR code:

www.familyvalued.org/Doreen-Amlung-2

Simone Rüssel

Alternative Practitioner for Psychotherapy

Germany

Parents-, sons- and daughters-in-law — 6 tips for better relations

Abstract

In this article I would like to encourage both parents- and sons/daughters-in-law to look at any difficulties they may have from a different perspective; and show some ways of dealing with them. Getting along together – and harmony between the generations – are important for every family and will make it stronger.

Article

There are so many mother-in-law jokes that I've often wondered why it's always the mothers-in-law who come off so badly. I don't know a single father-in-law joke. What is special about the mother-in-law-child-in-law connection? And the older I get the more likely it is that I too will become a mother-in-law one day. So, I ask myself, what can or should I do to become a "good" mother-in-law. Both in consultations in my practice and my private life I have been able to gain valuable insights on this subject.

First of all, it must be noted that there have always been generational conflicts. Aristotle said in the 4th century BC: "Our youth is unbearable, irresponsible and horrible to look at." Mutual understanding between the older and the younger generations is often limited. Every generation thinks it is doing things right. Changes towards new ways of life, and the acceptance of the experience of older generations – both seem suspect and inappropriate to the other's way of life. It is therefore not surprising that conflicts between parents of (small) children and grandparents are often sparked by the topic of upbringing. Especially in this area there is now a lack of consensus on what is important in upbringing and how these goals should be implemented. Things that used to be standard rules (e.g. stay at the table until everyone is finished, "You eat what is put in front of you.", give up your seat to older people in the tram, etc.), now often yields to the individual upbringing of children depending on the situation (e.g. if a child does not feel like sitting at the table until everyone is finished, it is allowed to get down. If it wants to remain, it can sit at the table until the adults also leave.)

It is not a question of preferring one path to the other. However, these examples show that differences in upbringing can be large and can meet with mutual incomprehension. On the subject of raising children, this could be one reason why there are more tensions between mothers-in-law and daughters-in-law, because despite efforts to involve fathers more in the upbringing, the main responsibility – at least in infancy – still seems to lie with the mothers. However, this does not mean that there can't be problems between fathers- and sons-in-law. Other sensitive topics are, for example: the mother's employment, dealing with the media, understanding the role of a father, etc.

"Just come to some arrangement yourselves."

For many women, the role of mother also means taking care of others, especially one's own children. Mothers-in-law sometimes fail to realize when it is important to give adult, married children more space. Too much interference is perceived as intrusive by children-in-law. It is very likely well-intentioned on the part of the mother-in-law; she just wanted to "take care", to give the benefit of her experience or do someone "a favour". What is experienced as overreach on one side is seen as disregard or contempt for experience on the part of the older generation. An objective discussion of these different assessments is often not possible because emotions quickly boil over on both sides. These situations are made even worse if the spouse – and in this case it more often the man – takes an indifferent position between his wife and his own mother ("Just come to some arrangement yourselves.") or sees himself still very much beholden to his own mother and tries to protect her ("She only means well."). Sooner or later this behaviour leads to great tensions in the marriage. I therefore always advise the married couples in my coaching sessions that the husband stands clearly by his wife and supports her. He can lovingly make it clear to his mother that she does not need to "take care of things". What is important here is that he show some appreciation for the supposed help.

On the other hand, I advise the parents-in-law that they need to hold back and wait for help to be requested, even if it is difficult. It has proven to be a good idea to establish that the rules of the host family prevail in a household, i.e. the rules of the parents-in-law prevail in their own home, while the rules of the son- and daughter-in-law apply in their own home. For the young children this may be confusing at first, but children are generally used to different rule sets: at kindergarten and school there are also different rules than at home.

In summary, I would like to give 6 tips for children-in-law and parents-in-law:
1)   Mutual appreciation and recognition are the basis for every good relationship. Do not neglect these, whatever other differences there may be.
2)   Trust that everyone wants to do everything they do as well as they can. Opinions about what is good and appropriate can vary, however.
3)   Address opposing views openly and, if possible, without aggression, i.e. do not wait too long to talk them over.
4)   For sons- and daughters-in-law: Express your appreciation and gratitude to your parents-in-laws for their life's work. However, also make it clear where your boundaries are, and that these must be observed by the in-laws.
5)   For parents-in-law: Many experiences simply cannot be passed on; they must be learned anew by each generation.

6)   Sometimes holding back, a little from your son- and daughter-in-law leads to greater closeness, even if this sounds paradoxical. Love needs freedom.

More information about the author via the QR code:

www.familyvalued.org/Simone-Ruessel-2